CATCHING
YELLOWSTONE'S
Wild Trout

CATCHING
YELLOWSTONE'S
Wild Trout

A FLY-FISHING HISTORY & GUIDE

CHRIS HUNT

FOREWORD BY MIKE SEPELAK

THE
History
PRESS

Published by The History Press
Charleston, SC
www.historypress.com

Front cover: photo by Chris Hunt.
Back cover: all photos by Chris Hunt.

First published 2019

ISBN 9781540239266

Library of Congress Control Number: 2019935352

PRAISE FOR
Catching Yellowstone's Wild Trout

I know a lot of writers, but I don't know of anyone who has actually fished in Yellowstone more than Chris Hunt. I've also read a lot of guide books on Yellowstone, which, as the crown jewel of our national parks (especially for the fly angler), deserves the attention. But this book is unique in that it isn't about just dividing the park into quadrants and mapping out where to go. Rather, in here you'll find deeper, far better species-driven substance, and you'll understand the "why" as much as you do the "what" or "where." Sure, you'll get the clear blueprint of where to go, and what to use. But fishing for trout is ultimately a game of figuring out the "why," and nobody has ever tackled that with greater aplomb or more effect. If you're really serious about fishing and fully enjoying what Yellowstone has to offer, there is no better, more credible resource than this book.

—KIRK DEETER, EDITOR-IN-CHIEF, *TROUT MAGAZINE*

You'll have no trouble finding guide books to help put you on trophy fish on Yellowstone's most fabled waters, or books that will tell you which rivers and streams hold which species of fish and how big they are. You'll even find books out there that will take you far into the Yellowstone's backcountry in search of unpressured fish far from other anglers and the park's hordes of car-dwelling sightseers. And you'll find any number of books that explore Yellowstone's storied history. But it's unlikely that, other than Catching Yellowstone's Wild Trout, *you'll find another volume that does all of those things at once. Chris Hunt, who has been fishing Yellowstone National Park for the better part of two decades (and who also happens to be one of fly-fishing's most insightful, talented and entertaining voices), has assembled what is perhaps the most complete and useful resource on fishing Yellowstone that you'll encounter anywhere—and one that will leave you with a rich, meaningful understanding of the park and its wild trout. Oh, and, if you must know...where to catch them.*

—CHAD SHMUKLER, EDITOR AND PUBLISHER, *HATCH MAGAZINE*

To Declan…let's go fishing one day soon, nephew.

Camping just outside the park near Cave Falls.
Photo by Rachel Andona.

Contents

Foreword

C hris sat at the wheel of the gray Nissan Titan, I rode shotgun and the three Yellowstone first-timers were shoehorned into the cramped back seat, their noses pressed to the windows as we drove the 142 miles of the Grand Loop.

We stopped at the waterfalls, grand and small. We pulled aside as herds of bison crossed the park's roadways, surrounding us in wooly wonder. We stretched our legs in lush high meadows, strode through the deep, drying grasses that gently swayed in warm, late summer breezes and sent grasshoppers chittering off in all directions. We played good tourists. It was absolute torture.

Torture, you ask? How could wandering through our country's greatest natural treasure, our first and best national park, be remotely considered torture?

Here's the thing. As we drove alongside iconic rivers, as we passed over innumerable creeks of all sizes, as we skirted the immense Yellowstone Lake, Chris pointed upstream or down and talked about what lies within and beyond our view from the pavement. He described in depth each waterway, told of its character and its history, recounted his years roaming its edges and, most vividly, detailed its inhabitants, the living jewels of Yellowstone National Park: its trout.

Chris was playing good host. He was being an excellent tour guide, but his narratives on the waters and their denizens were killing me. We had the day and only that day, for I was flying back East the next morning. The fly rods

were securely packed away. Torture? Yes, indeed, as we had no time to dig the 4- and 5-weight rods back out. No time to go and get lost in Yellowstone's stunning backcountry.

No time to fish.

I've had the great pleasure to travel with Chris all over this continent and beyond. We've chased magnificent roosterfish along the Mexican Baja and the Sea of Cortez, huge waterwolf pike in the wilds of northern Saskatchewan, lowly and misunderstood bowfin in the black backwaters of Georgia's Okefenokee Swamp and splinters of silver lightning, bonefish, in the sun-soaked Bahamas. His enthusiasm for our sport and his fly-fishing knowledge is broad and infectious, and I've been lucky to have experienced it, firsthand, in myriad far-flung destinations.

ABOVE: A classic "bison jam" in Hayden Valley. *Photo by Chris Hunt.*

OPPOSITE: The view as the Yellowstone River leaps over a 308-foot cliff at Lower Yellowstone Falls. *Photo by Chris Hunt.*

But I've come to learn that nowhere is Chris's wealth of experience and joy more deeply rooted than in his own corner of the world, his eastern Idaho and western Montana haunts, and it's at its core when he's chasing his real loves—his brookies, his browns, his rainbows and his cutthroats. Nowhere is he more in his element than when he's trout fishing in the American West.

You hold in your hand a distillation of that passion and an encyclopedia of location-specific fly-fishing knowledge. You've opened the pages of a personal recital of decades of Yellowstone angling experience—the "wheres," the "hows" and the "whats"—stitched together with firsthand stories that, let's all admit, are far more interesting and important than the fishing technicalities themselves. You ride shotgun in the Titan on your own tour of the park with Chris in the driver's seat as your guide. Luckily, you have the opportunity to spend more than a single day with him. Rest assured, for you, this time, it won't be torture.

—*Mike Sepelak, author, www.mikesgonefishing.com*

Acknowledgements

T hanks so much to Dr. Todd Koel, the lead fisheries biologist at Yellowstone National Park, and his team, including Annelise Ringelman, not only for their help with checking my information and making sure I sound like I know what I'm talking about, but also for their leadership over the last several years in crafting Yellowstone's thoughtful and science-based Native Fish Conservation Plan. This foresighted and science-based document has done wonders in the last eight years to restore and recover some of Yellowstone's imperiled fisheries treasures by providing a solid, workable and reasonable roadmap for native fish recovery, restoration and protection. Everyone who fishes Yellowstone National Park owes Todd a great debt of gratitude.

Another debt of gratitude goes out to perhaps the most selfless Trout Unlimited volunteer I've encountered in nearly fifteen years of working for TU: Dave Sweet. Dave has been active in the East Yellowstone chapter of Trout Unlimited for years, and much of the funding raised to help the National Park Service monitor and collect data on nonnative lake trout in Yellowstone Lake is due to Dave's tireless efforts to engage TU volunteers from Wyoming, Idaho, Montana and, frankly, all over the country. TU does not have a nationally funded campaign in Yellowstone—it is solely driven by volunteers who have worked to raise hundreds of thousands of dollars over the years to purchase telemetry equipment that has provided needed information to park service biologists. This information is used to tell biologists where to stretch gillnets, where the invasive lake trout might

be spawning and what corridors of the lake the big predators use over the course of time.

Thanks to this data, the park service, in the near future, can start targeting lake trout where they spawn and actually remove the fish at the egg and larval stage rather than targeting adult fish—this will go a long way toward recovering this vital native trout fishery. And, to think that so much has been done simply out of the goodness of Dave Sweet's heart, and the hearts and wallets of TU volunteers in the region and all over America. Well, that's amazing.

Thanks, too, to a true Yellowstone treasure, Craig Mathews, who can always be counted on to share quality information from his place near the counter at Blue Ribbon Flies in West Yellowstone, Montana, about the park and its fisheries—a topic he's forgotten more about than most will ever know. I never told Craig I was doing book research—this was a project late in happening. Nevertheless, he was quick to help with everything from directions, fly suggestions and fishing technique instructions every single time I asked him. Fly shop proprietors around the world could take a lesson from this gracious man.

Finally, thanks to Rachel Andona, my fishing buddy on many of these Yellowstone adventures. She possesses an unparalleled patience, a sense of infinite curiosity and offers me a friendship I will likely find nowhere else.

OPPOSITE, TOP: A marmot checks out anglers as they hike up the Fall River. *Photo by Chris Hunt.*

OPPOSITE, BOTTOM: Volunteers prepare to remove invasive lake trout from Yellowstone Lake. Lake trout are native to the Great Lakes and the Precambrian lakes of Canada. *Photo by Chris Hunt.*

Introduction

When John Colter set out from Manuel's Fort at the mouth of the Big Horn River in the fall of 1807 and wandered south and east into what is now Yellowstone National Park, things were quite a bit different than they are today.

Colter, widely believed to be the first European American to set foot in what is now the park, first documented the thermal features outside the east boundary of the park—an area that earned the nickname "Colter's Hell." While historical accounts of Colter's journey vary widely, he is largely credited for being the first white man to visit. He was initially part of the Lewis and Clark Corps of Discovery, whose travels to the Pacific are much better documented.

Think back to what Yellowstone may have been like, to the country Colter might have seen. No roads. Trails? Only those traveled infrequently by American Indians in the region and the game they pursued (native peoples have been using the park's unique resources for about eleven thousand years). The mighty Yellowstone River would have been an impassable torrent in most places (or, by the time he got there—if he really did—it may have been frozen under a foot of ice). Other great rivers, like the Snake, the Firehole, the Gibbon and the Madison, would have been truly wild, sporting only native fish—or no fish at all.

Yellowstone Lake would have looked like an inland sea, and access around its shores, with the many hot spots and hot springs, would have been

OPPOSITE: A bison enjoys a summer day near Biscuit Basin. *Photo by Chris Hunt.*

TOP: The Northern Lights make a rare appearance in Yellowstone, near Cave Falls late one May evening. *Photo by Rachel Andona.*

BOTTOM: Mountain whitefish are most closely related to Arctic grayling. *Photo by Chris Hunt.*

intimidating, to say the least. Other massive lakes, like Lewis and Shoshone on the western side of the park, would have been equally challenging to navigate.

And the fish in Yellowstone? All native. All wild. All exactly where they belonged. Today, after generations of nonnative fish management through the 1950s, the park's fisheries are quite a bit different than they were when Colter would have wandered through the park. There were no rainbow trout. No brook trout or lake trout. And no brown trout, either. In fact, the park's waters would have been inhabited by just three native salmonids—cutthroat trout, Arctic grayling and mountain whitefish.

And those fishy lakes and rivers of today? Lewis and Shoshone Lakes would have been completely fishless, as would have been the Firehole River above Firehole Falls. The Madison and the Gibbon would have contained native strains of west slope cutthroat trout, whitefish and Arctic grayling, all native to the headwaters of the Missouri River.

Yellowstone Lake would have been home solely to native Yellowstone cutthroat trout, whitefish and the native dace and suckers that continue to live there today. There would have been no lake trout in any of the park's waters—these nonnative predators weren't introduced into Yellowstone until 1890, and only then into Shoshone and Lewis Lakes (and later into Heart Lake).

This may have been one of the greatest tragedies in the park's biological history—invasive lake trout found their way into Yellowstone Lake in the late 1980s or early 1990s and nearly wiped out the legendary native cutthroats of the park's signature lake by the mid-2000s. Only diligence on behalf of the National Park Service, a volunteer effort from local Trout Unlimited chapters and the help of other nonprofit groups like the Greater Yellowstone Coalition and Yellowstone Forever have reduced the numbers of lake trout in Yellowstone Lake to enable the native cutthroats to make a reasonable comeback.

How did they get there? It could have been the nefarious deeds of an angler or two who wanted to spice up the fishing in Yellowstone Lake by illegally transplanting lake trout from Lewis or Shoshone Lakes. It could have happened in 1988, during the torrential and tragic fire season, when buckets of water from lake trout–infested waters were used to douse fires near Yellowstone Lake. Or it could have happened somewhat naturally—nonnative lake trout that wash out of Jackson Lake Dam in nearby Grand Teton National Park could have migrated up Pacific Creek to Two Ocean Creek to the famous "Parting of the Waters" and then to Atlantic Creek, which eventually dumps into the Yellowstone River in the wild and remote Thorofare region.

Yellowstone National Park fisheries biologist Todd Koel is investigating this possibility. In July 2018, Koel told the Associated Press, "There's surface water that connects up Two Ocean Pass, the waters of the Pacific drainage and the Atlantic drainage. I flew it last year and it was an open system, all the way to the top."

You might think, "Hey, a fish is a fish is a fish. What difference does it make if it's a cutthroat or a lake trout?"

The short answer? A big difference.

Cutthroats and lakers don't share the same habitat. Native cutthroats spawn in rivers and streams and, while they will venture deep, can often be caught near the surface. This means they aren't readily available only to anglers, but also to grizzly bears and black bears, eagles and ospreys, otters and mink—even wolves, coyotes and foxes have been documented chasing and eating Yellowstone cutthroat trout.

Lake trout, native to Canada and the upper Midwest, spawn in the lakes and spend the majority of their lives in very deep water. They are not a ready food source for the park's fish-eating predators.

The result? A jacked-up ecosystem. Bears that once keyed in on cutthroat trout in the spring were forced to go after elk and bison calves. Bald eagles now target trumpeter swan cygnets, young white pelicans, cormorants and ducks, and they're depending more on scavenged carcasses than they are on trout. What's more, since the cutthroat crash, nesting success for bald eagles is down significantly. Ospreys all but disappeared from the shores of Yellowstone Lake, and the few nesting pairs that do remain travel as far away as five air miles to find fish in other drainages. The loss of Yellowstone's namesake trout has reverberated throughout the food chain.

Several years ago, while attending a western regional meeting of Trout Unlimited in Jackson Hole, Wyoming, local TU chapter members "sticker-bombed" my truck with a telling bumper sticker. "Lake trout kill elk," the sticker read. And, if you consider how intertwined Yellowstone's predators are with its native fish, that statement is entirely correct. It could just as easily be said that "lake trout kill swans," or "lake trout kill ducks." In Yellowstone, everything is connected. And invasive lake trout tug at those connections, pulling at loose threads in the park's ecological fabric.

The somewhat sketchy accounts of Colter's visit to the region don't document the park's native fish—old John was a renowned hunter, but if he fished, there's no record of it in the park. What is known is that the fly-fishing paradise we all know Yellowstone National Park to be today was

A nice brown trout from Lewis River Channel. *Photo by Chris Hunt.*

about 40 percent fishless when the region was designated as the world's first national park in 1872.

It's not unreasonable to think that, because of the efforts to introduce trout to many previously barren waters in Yellowstone, the fishing is actually better today than it was when the park was created.

But it's a double-edged sword, as is the case in nearly every instance where nonnative fish are introduced into waters where they don't belong. Browns and rainbows, not cutthroat trout and grayling, now inhabit the storied Madison. Brook trout, which were the first nonnative salmonid to be introduced in the park in 1889, according to the National Park Service, when they were stocked in the upper Firehole River, are now widely dispersed throughout Yellowstone and have pushed native cutthroat trout out of headwater streams in nearly every region in the park.

Stocking of nonnative fish in Yellowstone continued into the 1950s, when the practice was stopped—by the 1930s, park managers had seen a noticeable decline in native trout and grayling thanks to nonnative introductions. Today, the only fish purposely stocked in the park are native trout that are being reintroduced to their historic waters, and not for the direct benefit of anglers (but that benefit exists, nonetheless).

Today, fishing in and around Yellowstone can still be quite good. Even though Yellowstone's annual visitation numbers topped four million in 2015 and have remained steady since, only about fifty thousand people fish in Yellowstone every year (and I would venture that the vast majority of those anglers are fly-fishers). The iconic trout rivers of Yellowstone, first made famous a century ago, are, for the most part, still excellent trout fisheries today. The chance to catch trophy trout of nearly every species available in the park—both native and nonnative—still exists. But, generally, Yellowstone is populated with small- to average-sized trout that offer great sport in one of the most impressive and unusual settings on earth. Only in Yellowstone can an angler cast to brown and rainbow trout as bison cross the river above or below them. Only here can a fly-fisher cast to trout as geysers gush boiling water from the beating heart of the planet into the same river.

For the cost of a park fishing license and the gate entrance fee, anglers can experience one of the most raw landscapes in the world, sliced from end to end by fabled roadside rivers and little-known (and little-fished) backcountry trout streams. It may only be here where anglers can spend half a day casting to brown trout native to Loch Leven in Scotland, and then travel twenty minutes to cast to Arctic grayling and west slope cutthroat trout that are once again swimming exactly where they belong. Then, they could finish off the day with a short drive and catch brookies native to Appalachia or a rainbow trout that sports the genetics from its native McCloud River in California.

There's only one Yellowstone. And, while not all of its fish belong there, they all share one thing in common. They're wild. Just like the park itself.

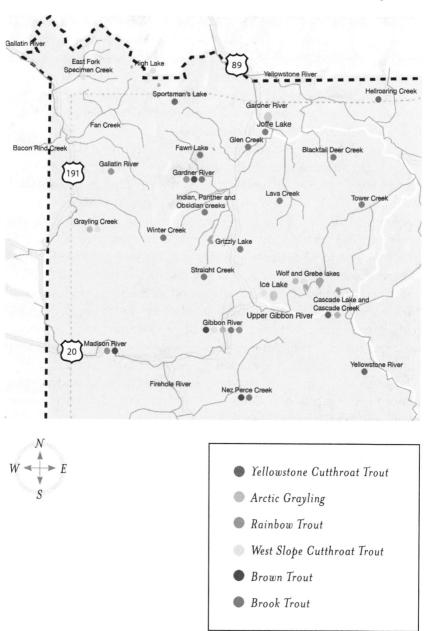

Gallatin River
East Fork Specimen Creek
High Lake
89
Yellowstone River
Hellroaring Creek
Sportsman's Lake
Gardner River
Joffe Lake
Fan Creek
Glen Creek
Bacon Rind Creek
Fawn Lake
Blacktail Deer Creek
191
Gallatin River
Gardner River
Indian, Panther and Obsidian creeks
Lava Creek
Tower Creek
Grayling Creek
Winter Creek
Grizzly Lake
Straight Creek
Wolf and Grebe lakes
Ice Lake
Cascade Lake and Cascade Creek
Upper Gibbon River
Gibbon River
20
Madison River
Yellowstone River
Firehole River
Nez Perce Creek

N
W ← → E
S

Legend:
- Yellowstone Cutthroat Trout
- Arctic Grayling
- Rainbow Trout
- West Slope Cutthroat Trout
- Brown Trout
- Brook Trout

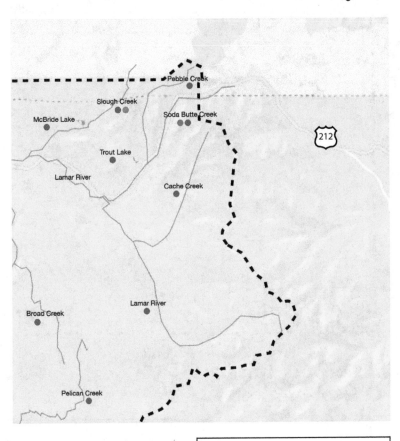

Pebble Creek

Slough Creek

McBride Lake

Soda Butte Creek

Trout Lake

Lamar River

Cache Creek

Lamar River

Broad Creek

Pelican Creek

212

● *Yellowstone Cutthroat Trout*

● *Rainbow Trout*

● *Brook Trout*

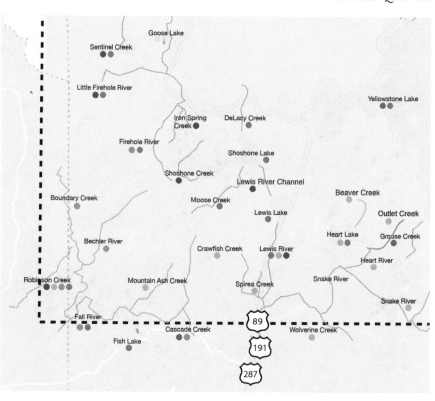

Goose Lake

Sentinel Creek

Little Firehole River

Yellowstone Lake

Iron Spring Creek   DeLacy Creek

Firehole River

Shoshone Lake

Shoshone Creek

Lewis River Channel

Beaver Creek

Boundary Creek

Moose Creek

Lewis Lake

Outlet Creek

Bechler River

Heart Lake   Grouse Creek

Crawfish Creek   Lewis River

Heart River

Robinson Creek

Mountain Ash Creek

Spirea Creek   Snake River

Snake River

Fall River

89

Cascade Creek   Wolverine Creek

Fish Lake

191

287

● *Yellowstone Cutthroat Trout*

● *Snake River Fine-Spotted Cutthroat Trout*

● *Rainbow Trout*

● *West Slope Cutthroat Trout*

● *Brown Trout*

● *Brook Trout*

● *Lake Trout*

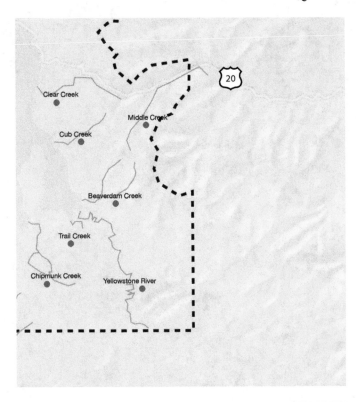

● *Yellowstone Cutthroat Trout*

1
A Little History

Several of today's iconic fisheries in Yellowstone National Park are only fisheries thanks to the graces of the U.S. Army, which managed the park from 1886 until 1918. The army was called in to manage the park, largely because Yellowstone's unique geologic and environmental resources were under attack from opportunists—its wildlife was poached, hot springs were used as laundry facilities for tourist encampments, archaeological and unique geological relics were removed and so forth.

Without funding from Congress to protect the park's resources, the job fell to the army. And, in the park's early years, there was a desire on the part of the park's European American administrators to enhance the fishing in Yellowstone. In fact, Captain Frazier Boutelle, who managed the park from 1888 to 1891, was quoted as saying, "I hope to see all of these waters so stocked that the pleasure-seeker in the Park can enjoy fine fishing within a few rods of any hotel or camp."

The army and the U.S. Fish Commission (which later became the U.S. Fish and Wildlife Service) set about trying to meet that goal, with generally successful results. Remember, not much, if anything, was known about Yellowstone's native trout—cutthroat trout, whitefish and grayling—and, in fact, these fish were often viewed with disdain. One of the early—and, thankfully, unsuccessful—efforts to stock nonnative fish in the park was when, in 1908 and 1909, a total of twelve thousand landlocked Atlantic salmon were introduced in Yellowstone Lake. Another two thousand salmon were introduced to Duck Lake in 1909. Landlocked Atlantic salmon depend

Jay Astle and Jim Duke fish Yellowstone's Firehole River. *Photo by Chris Hunt.*

on forage fish for their diet—that's largely a missing element in Yellowstone, as there aren't really large schools of baitfish in any of the park's lakes. This could explain why, thankfully, these fish never became established.

Other unusual stocking efforts included largemouth bass, 250 of which were planted in the Gibbon River in 1893, and another 500 were planted in various lakes in 1896. Not surprisingly, given Yellowstone's harsh winters and year-round cold waters, bass didn't do very well. As of 1912, they were deemed gone from the park, with a recommendation that they not be planted again.

"This fish does not harmonize with trouts, and its predatory habits make it an unsafe species to introduce into these waters," wrote W.C. Kendall, an assistant with the U.S. Bureau of Fisheries, in *The Fishes of Yellowstone National Park*, first published in 1914 and updated in 1921 by Hugh M. Smith. That's certainly true—bass are, indeed, predators. But their lack of success in Yellowstone was almost certainly due to environmental conditions, not because they were considered undesirable, at least when they were introduced.

The Kendall/Smith report is the first effort at detailing fish stocking in the park, but it covers only the first forty years or so of fisheries management in Yellowstone. A second, more updated report, done by fisheries biologist John D. Varley and published in 1981 (*A History of Fish Stocking Activities in Yellowstone National Park Between 1881 and 1980*), is the report used today by park service biologists, and it includes stocking efforts through 1959, when all nonnative fish-stocking efforts in the park ceased.

There are other disparate records of stocking efforts in Yellowstone, ranging from carp to yellow perch (which were discovered in 1919 in Goose Lake near the Firehole River). As of today, all stockings, save for those of rainbow, brown, brook and lake trout, were unsuccessful. And that's a good thing—fishing today in Yellowstone is what it is because of the park's native and naturalized wild trout. No nonnative trout—or any other fish, for that matter—has been stocked in Yellowstone's waters since 1959.

Further, the nonnative fish that thrive in the park today have been in Yellowstone's waters for well over a century. Consider the following:

RAINBOW TROUT, presumably from the McCloud River in California, according to the Kendall/Smith report, were first stocked in Grebe Lake in the Gibbon River drainage in 1889. The updated version of the 1914 report released in 1921 indicates that rainbows may have been introduced above Virginia Cascade on the Gibbon as early as 1880, but that seems early, given that most other nonnative fish weren't introduced into the park for almost another decade. The Varley report claims rainbows weren't introduced into Grebe Lake until 1909, just one of the many discrepancies between the two reports.

LOCH LEVEN BROWN TROUT, native to Scotland, were first stocked in 1889, when 995 fish were planted in the Firehole River above Firehole Falls.

VON BEHR BROWN TROUT were first planted in 1890, when 9,800 of the German-strain browns named after Baron Lucius von Behr, the president of the German Fishing Society, were planted in Nez Perce Creek, a tributary to the Firehole. Von Behr brown trout were also the first browns introduced to the United States when they were imported by a New York fish farmer in 1883.

LAKE TROUT, native to the Great Lakes and Canada, were introduced, according to Kendall's report, only once in the park's history. About 42,000 fish were planted in Shoshone and Lewis Lakes in 1890. (They now thrive in Heart Lake, too.) A separate claim by Yellowstone historian

Hiram Chittenden (the namesake of Chittenden Bridge over the Yellowstone River) made in 1914 that lake trout were introduced into the Yellowstone River above Yellowstone Falls in 1890 is likely not accurate—the fish weren't observed in Yellowstone Lake until 1994.

The National Park Service reports that eastern brook trout were first introduced into the Firehole River in 1889; Kendall's report claims they were introduced into the Gardiner River, also in 1889. The updated version of the 1914 report claims that the park superintendent documented brookies in Shoshone Creek, a tributary to Shoshone Lake, in 1887. Throughout the late 1800s and early 1900s, brookies were introduced into dozens of rivers and streams throughout the park. Today, they might be the most widely distributed sport fish in Yellowstone.

According to Koel, the park's lead fisheries biologist, more than 300 million fish were stocked in Yellowstone from the late 1800s through 1959. Given these introductions, one could surmise that we're lucky we have any native trout at all left in Yellowstone today.

In 2010, the National Park Service embarked on an ambitious plan to restore native trout to their native waters within Yellowstone National Park. The park's Native Fish Conservation Plan, developed by Koel and many of his colleagues with the park service and other federal agencies, lays out a roadmap for native trout recovery in Yellowstone.

Not only does it address the ongoing effort to reduce lake trout (complete removal is likely impossible) from Yellowstone Lake, but it also addresses other native trout and the challenges they face within the park's boundaries. For instance, in Yellowstone's northwest corner, the native cutthroat trout is the west slope cutthroat. For years, these fish were thought to have been eradicated within the park, thanks mostly to nonnative trout introductions. But two relict populations of these fish were located in very small streams within the park, and the progeny of these "rediscovered" fish are being used to reintroduce native trout to several Missouri River headwater streams inside Yellowstone.

OPPOSITE, TOP: A nice brook trout falls for a hopper on the upper reaches of the Little Firehole River. *Photo by Chris Hunt.*

OPPOSITE, BOTTOM: Todd Koel, the lead fisheries biologist, shows journalists how the National Park Service is working to reduce the numbers of invasive lake trout in Yellowstone Lake. *Photo by Chris Hunt.*

Netting and removing invasive lake trout from Yellowstone Lake. *Photo by Chris Hunt.*

Grayling, too, were once abundant in the Gibbon, Madison, Gallatin and lower Firehole Rivers, according to Kendall's 1914 report. Today, efforts to reintroduce native Arctic grayling into the headwater lakes and streams of the Gibbon and Madison Rivers, Missouri River tributaries where grayling are native, are underway.

As Koel wrote in 2017, "Native fish cannot fulfill their ecological role in [Yellowstone National Park] if their populations are extirpated or remain decimated, hybridized and isolated."

That's largely the message of the Native Fish Conservation Plan. Much of Yellowstone's ecosystem, when viewed at the thirty-thousand-foot level, depends on trout and the ability for predators to get to them. While some introduced trout can, for the most part, fulfill the role of the native trout they've replaced—an osprey or a mink will eat a brown trout, just as it will eat a cutthroat trout—that's not true in every situation. A healthy, intact fishery with a robust presence of native trout is important to the future of Yellowstone, and not just from a fishing perspective.

As Koel wrote in "An Approach to Conservation of Native Fish in Yellowstone," an article published by the National Park Service in 2017, fisheries managers within the park are taking an active role in reintroducing and bolstering native fish populations in lakes and streams where those actions are both economical and likely to achieve success. The goal, as stated in the 2010 Native Fish Conservation Plan, is to prevent the long-term possibility of extinction of the park's native fish—west slope and Yellowstone cutthroat trout and fluvial (migrating between lakes and rivers) Arctic grayling.

What exactly does that mean? Will we lose our beloved browns that cruise the thermally enhanced pools of the Firehole? The trophy rainbows from the upper Bechler? The spunky little brookies from Obsidian Creek or the upper Gardner River?

Almost certainly, the answer is no. Yellowstone will always be home to the fish that are now truly naturalized to the environment. There will always be lake trout and brown trout in Lewis and Shoshone Lakes. Brookies will likely always be found in Indian Creek, where kids can get at them and feel that tug of a wild fish on light tackle. And rainbows and browns will always run up the Madison from Hebgen Lake to spawn.

But where it's possible, the park service should do what it can to restore native trout in Yellowstone. It's not only good for the fish and the park's ecosystem, but it's also good for those of us who chase them. Fishing in Yellowstone is a visceral experience—it's so wonderfully unique. Making the habitat whole and intact again, at least as much as possible, is the right thing to do, and any angler worth his or her salt would much rather experience the park in as close to its natural state as can be.

And we can do our part by following Yellowstone's progressive fishing regulations. All native fish—cutthroats, grayling and whitefish—must be released. Anglers catching lake trout in Yellowstone and Heart Lakes *must* kill their catch.

Everyone has a role in making fishing better in Yellowstone. The first step, though, is understanding that native trout and grayling play as vital a role in the park's ecosystem as other, more gregarious critters, like grizzly bears, wolves, elk and bison. In fact, the role of Yellowstone's native trout is vital to the survival of all the animals listed above—they are a foundational element of the park's complex food web.

Returning native fish to the park not only provides anglers with more fishing opportunities, it also increases the health and resiliency of the park in the face of growing challenges, like markedly increased human visitation, climate change and all its trappings, as well as the growth and expansion of gateway communities.

Americans love their national parks for all they offer. Taking care of our first national park so future generations can experience it and marvel in its wonders is important. For anglers, working to protect and enhance Yellowstone's native fish is how we can do our part.

2

Some Tips for Fishing Yellowstone National Park

First and foremost, it's your responsibility as an angler to know and follow the fishing regulations put forth by the National Park Service. You'll need a Yellowstone-specific fishing license, which—along with a copy of the most up-to-date regulations—is available at most fly shops in gateway communities like West Yellowstone, Gardner, Jackson and Cody. Pay close attention to opening dates, particularly in native cutthroat country—cutthroats spawn in the spring, and the National Park Service keeps many cutthroat fisheries closed, sometimes into July and August, to protect spawning cutthroats.

Also of note, as of 2018, felt-soled wading boots are no longer permitted in the park. There are worries that the felt can serve to spread aquatic invasive species, like whirling disease and New Zealand mud snails (both of which, sadly, are already found in some park waters). Remember to pay attention to updates over the course of the summer—in hot summers, many of Yellowstone's rivers will be closed periodically to prevent stress to wild trout when rivers get too warm for their liking. Generally, when rivers reach seventy degrees, trout fishing is ceased. Water warmer than that can be deadly to trout, particularly if they're stressed by being caught and released.

Second, remember that you'll be fishing in the world's first national park. This place is special to a lot of people, and four million of us visit every year. Be kind. Be considerate. Give kids the right-of-way, particularly on roadside streams where access is easy. Don't approach wildlife—sometimes,

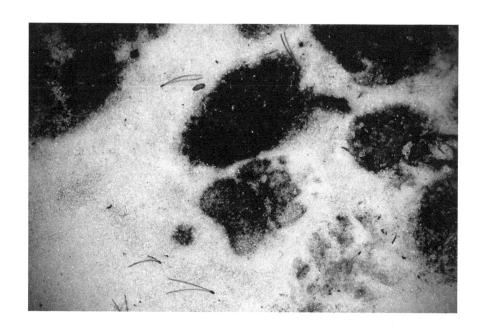

particularly in places like the Firehole or the Lamar Valleys, you may have to move around a bit to avoid getting too close to bison.

Third, remember this little bit of advice. The farther you get from the road, the better the fishing gets. Stretch your legs. Explore. Wander a trail along a small, alpine stream or bushwhack through the willows when you can. Most folks who visit Yellowstone don't leave sight of their vehicles (even though, for the most part, they can). Be a rogue—venture a bit into the backcountry. Chances are, you'll be by yourself and enjoy some really good fishing for wild trout.

But be safe. Bear spray is always a good idea. Have it, and know how to use it. Your chances of encountering a bear are slim, particularly if you make noise (I always find myself whistling the tune from the old World War II film *The Bridge on the River Kwai* when I'm fishing in bear country) and let bears you might not see know you're around.

In marshy areas with willows, be on the lookout for moose. Mothers with calves can be testy—don't get too close. The same applies, obviously, to bison, which inflict more injuries on Yellowstone tourists than any other animal.

Be aware of thermal features. Often, very hot, scalding water is located just under the crust near hot pools and hot springs. Watch where you're walking. Carry some basic first-aid gear if you can.

Before you venture down a trail, do some simple recon. Know where you're headed, what the trail will be like from an elevation-gain or elevation-loss perspective. Know how long it will take you to get where you're going (and how long it'll take to get back). Carry water (or at least water filtration equipment) and a snack or two for extended hikes. It's always a good idea to carry a small headlamp, just in case you get delayed and you're forced to walk out after dark.

I always like to plan my backcountry Yellowstone hikes by looking at the area I'm visiting using Google Earth or Google Maps. At the very least, consider keeping a copy of *De Lorme's Atlas and Gazetteer* for Wyoming in your car. The maps or satellite images will give you enough data to be largely familiar with your destination and the difficulty of the trail you're considering.

OPPOSITE, TOP: Hikers and bears share the DeLacy Creek Trail. *Photo by Rachel Andona.*

OPPOSITE, BOTTOM: A bull moose wanders the willows along the Snake River. *Photo by Chris Hunt.*

Finally, let someone know where you're headed. If you don't show up when you're supposed to, they can at least contact officials in the park who can come looking for you.

Yellowstone is a magical place, and a lot of people love it and visit often. With all the traffic you'll see on the roads, it may not seem like wild country. That's an incorrect assumption. Getting off the beaten path comes with risks—as I said, most folks don't do it. The few who do should always be prepared for the things that can go wrong.

Simply put, be smart. Don't take unnecessary chances. If you're wise, you'll get to experience many great trips into the Yellowstone backcountry.

OPPOSITE: One of the most iconic destinations in Yellowstone—Old Faithful geyser. *Photo by Chris Hunt.*

3
The Gear You'll Need

When I was a kid living in Colorado, I heard tales of massive trout hitting flies and coming to the net in Yellowstone National Park. And I have no doubt that some of those stories are true, particularly before the discovery of lake trout in Yellowstone Lake in 1994.

While it is certainly possible to catch big fish within Yellowstone's boundaries today, the average fish in the park, at least from a size perspective, is pretty unimpressive. Sure, a day's hike can put you on really big native cutthroats or backcountry browns, rainbows, brookies or lake trout, but most of the more accessible rivers, lakes and streams offer really good fly-fishing for trout ranging from just a few inches long to about seventeen inches—and the latter is rare.

When I fish Yellowstone, I almost always chase trout with light tackle. Native cutthroat streams can produce big trout, but even then, you're generally in pretty tight quarters. And many of Yellowstone's waters—even backcountry streams—have been overrun by nonnative brook trout that tend to be quite diminutive. For these waters, I rarely pull anything bigger than a 3-weight rod out of my truck.

That said, if you're interested in chasing big trout and willing to make the commitment to get to them, a 5-weight outfit should fit your needs nicely. On some of the park's bigger waters—like the Yellowstone, the Lamar, the lower Gibbon, Madison and Firehole Rivers—this is my rod of choice. Often, though, it's not because I'm going to be encountering really big fish, but because I'll be throwing more line and heavier flies.

A bull elk guards his harem on the Madison River. *Photo by Rachel Andona.*

Rarely do I use anything heavier than a 5-weight fly rod in the park. But, when chasing big browns in the Madison in the fall, or hiking into the Lewis River Channel in October to swing streamers for browns and lake trout, you might consider a 7-weight outfit (and I'd bring a sink-tip line so I can get deep fast). If you fish from a boat on Yellowstone or Lewis Lakes, you'll be glad for a bigger outfit that will help you cut the wind and throw more line at cruising fish.

Lines and reels should obviously correspond to your fly rod (though, if you're casting in the wind on the lower Lamar in August or September, you might overline a 5-weight rod with a 6-weight line).

As for waders, these are a virtual necessity early in the year and later in the season, as are wading boots (no felt, remember?). In high summer, I love to fish Yellowstone's smaller, higher waters in shorts and a pair of wading sandals or wading boots. Bright, warm sunny days in July and August are ideal for wet wading, and cool water against your shins is tough to beat when you're doused in sunscreen and sporting a hat, a Buff and maybe even some long sleeves. If you're not a fan of shorts, consider lightweight fishing pants that dry quickly and help keep you cool.

In some places in the park, wading can be a bit treacherous. If you're not as sturdy on your feet as you used to be, I'd recommend a wading staff and studded wading boots. It never hurts to play it safe.

I almost never use a net in the park, but I know that some anglers, particularly on bigger waters, like having one handy. If you do choose to use a net, consider a rubberized mesh that's a lot friendlier on trout than nylon or other mesh materials.

For the most part, leaders and tippets in Yellowstone's waters rarely need to be lighter than 4x. I find that going after trout with light tippet puts a lot of undue stress on fish as we enjoy the fight while trying not to break our 6x or even 7x tippet. As a rule, on cloudy days in the park, or if I'm swinging streamers, I'll go with 3x. On sunny days, I'll go with 4x. Anything lighter, in my opinion, is overkill and dangerous for fish, especially in the summer, when many of the park's thermally influenced rivers are warmer than when they are in the spring or fall. This could also help explain why I rarely use a net. And remember, keep your fish wet at all times. It's fine to pull a trout out of the water for a few seconds to snap that photo, but for the fish's sake, keep its out-of-the-water time to a minimum.

For flies, I've tried to give some ideas in later chapters that focus on the park's wild fish and the waters where they swim. Mostly, though, for small water, I'd fully stock a box of attractor dry flies. For lakes in the park, small streamers like Woolly Buggers, Zonkers, Slumpbusters and Muddlers will work well. Nymphs under indicators or high-floating dry flies can work well, and in lower-elevation streams in late summer, you should have your hopper box with you at all times. Lastly, don't forget soft-hackles—some of my best fishing days on the Firehole and Gibbon have come when I was swinging small soft-hackles. Remember, pinch your barbs. It just makes releasing fish easier.

Finally, a good supplement to this book is *Hiking Yellowstone National Park*, by my friend Bill Schneider. While I've attempted to include general directions to each destination, depending on the fish you're after, I usually only hike if there are fish at the end of the trail. Bill's book will give you some much-needed guidance on trails to the destinations I've outlined from here on out—complete with detailed distances and some other good information, like elevation changes, trail difficulty, etcetera.

Be safe. Be smart. Enjoy fishing Yellowstone. It should be a bucket-list trip for every fly-fisher.

4
Yellowstone Cutthroat Trout

or years, I've driven over the tiny trickle that is Cascade Creek en route to Canyon and the tourist havens at the upper and lower Yellowstone Falls. To me, these features are the most photogenic in all of Yellowstone—Old Faithful is nice, and the drive around the north and west edges of Yellowstone Lake is pretty cool, but, for me anyway, the waterfalls of Yellowstone are my favorite.

And Yellowstone Falls is the waterfall to beat all waterfalls. It helps, too, when I'm showing the park to friends and family, that we get some perspective. We first stop at Gibbon Falls, a stunning roadside attraction that looks like a natural waterslide. Then we take the little side road to Virginia Cascade, which is breathtaking.

And then we'll brave the throngs of visitors at the brink of the lower falls, where the Grand Canyon of the Yellowstone stretches out below us, and the emerald waters of the Yellowstone River suddenly drop over a 308-foot cliff right at our feet (that's twice the height of Niagara Falls, if you're scoring at home). On the drive out, we'll get a look at the lower falls from the downstream perspective—it's one of the most amazing scenes on earth. All told, I imagine I've spent dozens of hours soaking in the beauty of the falls with others in tow who are seeing them for the first time. Their reactions of awe and appreciation simply thrill me.

But at heart, I'm a fly-fisher. And the sexy little creek that crosses under the road between Norris and Canyon, not too far from the mighty Yellowstone itself, always made me wonder. It's a meadow stream that flows east from

tiny Cascade Lake, makes a southerly turn and winds its way all the way to the Yellowstone, where it enters the river between the upper and lower Yellowstone Falls.

Until recently, I'd never fished it, despite nearly two decades of promising myself to do just that. And when I finally did, I reaped the rewards.

I parked at the Cascade Trailhead west of Canyon, assembled a supple 2-weight glass rod, stuck a box full of small attractor patterns in my pocket and wandered off to see if Cascade Creek was worth the twenty-year wait.

Long story short, yes. It was. The little stream meanders among willows and through obsidian bluffs that can give anglers a great elevated perspective. It sports deep bends, long runs and soft tailouts that riffle their way to the next run or the next bend.

But, honestly, when I first got to the water, about a mile or so above where Cascade Creek flows under the highway, I was pretty sure I was going to spend an afternoon casting to six-inch trout. It's tiny water that requires stealth and tight casts—most anglers aren't too keen on working this hard to catch small trout.

And, yes, there are some small trout in Cascade Creek. But there are some larger trout, too. Sure, I caught my share of six-inch native Yellowstone cutthroat trout that afternoon, but I also caught a handful of foot-long cutties that put an appreciative bend in the fiberglass noodle I was using on the stream. It was early in the year, and the cutthroats, while not in full-on spring spawning regalia, were absolutely gorgeous. And every one of them hit dry flies with that typical cutthroat abandon—I don't believe backcountry cutthroat trout possess a timid gene.

What I eventually realized about Cascade's robust native cutthroats is that they might even be more special than the "native" moniker implies. Not only are they native fish that have likely been swimming in Cascade Creek since shortly after the last ice age, but they also could actually be somewhat genetically unique, given where Cascade enters the Yellowstone. There can't be any spawning recruitment from downstream, because the lower Yellowstone Falls is the mother of all fish barriers. The only "fresh"

OPPOSITE, TOP: A Yellowstone cutthroat trout from Cascade Creek. *Photo by Chris Hunt.*

OPPOSITE, BOTTOM: A cutthroat trout from Wolverine Creek in the southern reaches of Yellowstone. *Photo by Chris Hunt.*

genetic influence into Cascade would have to come from upstream, and those fish would have to survive the 108-foot drop over upper Yellowstone Falls. Possible, but unlikely.

I'm no biologist, but I like the idea that Cascade Creek's cutthroat trout aren't just native—they're *especially* native, and this little population of fish is found nowhere else on earth.

I worked my way back to the Norris-Canyon Road and eventually wandered back to the west to where I'd parked the car. As I walked, I got some curious stares from the passing motorists. It was as if they were asking, "He was fishing *that*? That tiny little stream? Are there even any fish in there?"

Let that be the lesson. In Yellowstone, nearly every small stream you see as it either parallels a road or crosses under one is potentially fishy. Just because you don't see other anglers fishing these waters doesn't mean they aren't worth fishing. In fact, it usually means just the opposite.

THE FISH

Yellowstone cutthroat trout are the signature native trout of Yellowstone National Park. They are found in the entire Yellowstone River drainage, from the headwaters of the Yellowstone River at Two Ocean Creek in Wyoming all the way downstream past Livingston, Montana.

Yellowstone cutthroat trout are found in dozens, if not hundreds, of waters within the Yellowstone National Park boundaries, including the tributaries of Yellowstone Lake, which is the last true big-water habitat for pure-strain Yellowstone cutthroat trout left in the world. This population is rebounding after a crash in the middle of the first decade of this century due to a nonnative lake trout invasion—the National Park Service and its conservation partners have worked for years to reduce the numbers of lake trout in Yellowstone Lake, largely by gillnetting and box-netting the predatory invasives that are native to the Great Lakes. Today, Yellowstone cutthroat trout are in recovery mode—they're found again in the headwaters of the Yellowstone River in the remote Thorofare region of Wyoming, just outside the park boundaries, and they are returning again in appreciative numbers to tributary streams all along Yellowstone Lake.

For the purpose of this book, I cover the Snake River fine-spotted cutthroat trout—a virtual genetic match with Yellowstone cutthroats—in a separate chapter. There is some debate about whether the Snake River variety of

The famed Second Meadow of Slough Creek just above where the creek dives into a long canyon. *Photo by Chris Hunt.*

cutthroats (which, in many waters in northern Wyoming and eastern Idaho, swim alongside their big-spotted cousins) deserve their own subspecies listing. I'll let the biologists sort it out. One thing is certain—the cutthroats in the Snake River drainage are separated from the park's Yellowstone cutthroats by the Continental Divide. For easy reference, the Snake River fine-spotted cutthroat trout is found in the southwest corner of Yellowstone, an area that includes the Pitchstone Plateau and is often called "Cascade Corner," due to the hundreds of waterfalls found on rivers and streams flowing off the plateau's slopes into the Snake, Fall and Henry's Fork Rivers.

Fishing for Yellowstone cutthroat trout is catch-and-release only. Streams entering Yellowstone Lake are closed until July 15 each year. Yellowstone Lake itself opens on June 15. There are several places along the Yellowstone River that are closed to fishing—be sure to check park fishing regulations before you go fishing.

THE BEST PLACES TO CATCH
YELLOWSTONE CUTTHROAT TROUT

The Yellowstone River

Located both above and below Yellowstone Lake, the river is home once again to robust populations of native Yellowstone cutthroat trout, thanks largely to the lake trout removal efforts conducted in Yellowstone Lake by the park service and its conservation partners. Again, remember that the Yellowstone River within the boundaries of Yellowstone National Park is closed to fishing until July 15 to protect spawning fish. Anglers can fish the river outside the park's boundaries in the Thorofare before that date, but that stretch of wild water requires a really long hike (some twenty-eight miles, one way) or horseback ride. The river below the lake to Yellowstone Falls opens on July 15, but it's closed a mile below and a quarter mile above Fishing Bridge year-round. Also, the river is closed one hundred yards above and below Lehardy Rapids.

The river below the falls in the Grand Canyon of the Yellowstone and farther downstream in the Black Canyon of the Yellowstone offers some of the best fishing for sizeable cutthroats in the park, but access can be tough—in many places, it's a thigh-busting hike to the bottom and a lung-busting hike back to the car.

FLIES: Early in the year, consider early-season mayflies, like Green Drakes, small caddis flies and, on warmer days, Pale Morning Duns and small golden stonefly imitations, like a Yellow Sally. For fishing in the canyon stretches below the falls, larger stonefly imitations will work well in early to mid-July, when water levels are high and fish are concentrated near the banks and in-stream structure. As water levels drop, go to more traditional dry flies (PMDs, Adams, Stimulators, etcetera). For nymphs on the upper section

OPPOSITE: The Grand Canyon of the Yellowstone from the lip of the Lower Yellowstone Falls. *Photo by Chris Hunt.*

The Yellowstone River flows northwest near Tower Junction, Yellowstone National Park. *Photo by Chris Hunt.*

below the lake, consider small golden stonefly nymphs and basic attractor nymphs, like a Prince or a bead-head pheasant tail. If you like to swing streamers, consider small (size 8–10) Woolly Buggers in black, brown and olive, or Slumpbusters in the same colors. In the canyon stretches, switch over to bigger streamers and bigger nymphs as summer goes on. Come August, don't venture to the river without a box full of hoppers.

Yellowstone Lake

The lake opens to fishing on June 15 (but, after really hard winters, the lake may still have ice on it then). Certain areas, like the shoreline along the West Thumb, are closed year-round, likely because of thermal features that make foot travel dangerous. No, the lake hasn't fully recovered from the lake trout infestation, but it's getting better. For shore-bound anglers, consider Gull Point

as your first stop. If you have a float tube, don't get too excited—Yellowstone Lake is huge, and if you're not careful, it can be dangerous. Stay close to shore. Anglers can rent boats at Bridge Bay Marina and travel farther to reach the lake's storied native trout—if you have the means, you can really improve your chances at catching big cutthroats, particularly early in the year, near creek inlets and over drop-offs. Look for structure and subsurface features. That's where fish will be found. Don't be afraid to "go big" on the lake—use a 7-weight to cut the wind, and don't hesitate to try a sink-tip line, particularly on sunny days, when fish will be holding in deeper water.

FLIES: Streamers are your best bet on Yellowstone Lake for native cutthroats, but occasionally, there will be mayfly hatches that bring big cutthroats to the top. I've had good luck using Adams in size 12 for these "gulpers" on the lake. These hatches are sporadic and generally occur in the evenings. If you find one, you'll have a blast.

The Lamar River

The Lamar River starts deep in the Absoroka backcountry south of Cooke City, Montana, and flows north into the fabled Lamar Valley of Yellowstone National Park. In its backcountry reaches—which will require a good hike through serious grizzly country—the fish are abundant, aggressive...and small. As the Lamar flows north, it's joined by Soda Butte Creek along the Northeast Entrance Road west of Cooke City, and it's a great place to catch good numbers of twelve- to fifteen-inch native Yellowstone cutthroat trout, with a chance at bigger fish as you go downstream toward the river's confluence with the Yellowstone just north of Tower Junction. The Lamar runs dirty throughout early summer with runoff from the high country—it usually doesn't clear up and become fishable until the middle of July. But when it does, it can be really good.

FLIES: When the river clears, consider going right to hoppers. Yes, there are other bugs that hatch on the Lamar, like Green Drakes and caddis, but often, it's the hoppers and other terrestrial flies that bring the bigger fish to the top. In lieu of hopper patterns, go with good, proven attractors, like Stimulators, Royal Coachmans, Madam Xs, Adams and so on. If you like to swing streamers, a black or olive Woolly Bugger will be hard to beat.

Slough Creek

Slough Creek flows south—southwest into Yellowstone National Park from Montana's Absoroka-Beartooth Wilderness. This is probably the best place in all of Yellowstone to catch trophy-sized native Yellowstone cutthroat trout. But you'll have to work for it. You can access the creek at the Slough Creek campground, but it gets hammered in its lower reaches. In order to get into really good fishing, it's almost vital to hike to one of four meadow stretches of the creek, with Third Meadow being the farthest from the campground, to Lower Meadow being the closest. Predictably, the fishing gets better the farther you go. It's six miles to Third Meadow, just over two miles to First Meadow and about four miles to Second Meadow. Lower Meadow is about a mile downstream to where Slough Creek meets the Lamar River.

Hiking into the meadows of Slough Creek. *Photo by Chris Hunt.*

FLIES: Two words: dry flies. Slough's cutthroat are big—a twenty-inch fish isn't unusual, and, when high summer hits, these fish are tuned into terrestrial flies. Bring your attractor box if you like, but I've had days in Second Meadow and Third Meadow when I never changed flies from the Dave's Hopper I started with.

Soda Butte Creek

Soda Butte Creek is named for a unique geologic formation near the eastern edge of the Lamar Valley, and it's another dependable location for Yellowstone cutthroat trout. It's also the site of a National Park Service restoration project—efforts are ongoing to remove nonnative brook trout from Soda Butte Creek, as brookies tend to out-compete native cutthroat trout. Nevertheless, it offers excellent fishing for small- to mid-sized

Lower Soda Butte Creek, Yellowstone National Park. *Photo by Chris Hunt.*

cutthroats from where it enters the park near the Northeast Entrance to where it comes together with the Lamar River near the Northeast Entrance Road several miles west of the actual Northeast Entrance. Higher up on Soda Butte, where it travels through heavy timber, the stream is basically a pocket water paradise populated by smaller cutthroats and the occasional brook trout. The farther west the stream flows (and the more streams it picks up—creeks like Pebble Creek and the tiny Amphitheater Creek), the larger it gets. Eventually, Soda Butte comes out of the timber and some deeper canyon stretches and becomes a full-fledged meadow stream, where some bigger cutthroats (twelve to fifteen inches or so) can be caught.

FLIES: Attractor patterns should work just fine, and lightweight tackle should do the trick in the timber reaches, where you'll be fishing pocket water. The lower reaches should be approached with larger attractors, like Stimulators and, early in the season, Yellow Sallies. Consider hoppers starting around the first week of August and fish them until a hard freeze, usually sometime in early September.

Middle Creek

Middle Creek runs along the East Entrance Road—the trout stream you'll see to the south of the road when you're either entering or exiting the park through the East Entrance is Middle Creek. It starts atop Sylvan Pass and flows east toward Cody. It eventually runs into the East Fork of the Shoshone River at Pahaska Teepee outside the park's boundaries. Inside the park, Middle Creek carries a good bit of water, and it flows through timber with lots of woody debris and good structure for native Yellowstone cutthroat trout. There are a number of pull-outs along the road that provide good access to Middle Creek and its generally eager native fish. While access is good, the fishing itself can be tough, and not because the fish aren't willing. There is a lot of structure in Middle Creek, and wading anglers should be careful around log jams, submerged boulders and the like. The best advice for Middle Creek? Let the runoff subside so you can better see the challenges you're facing—fish it in July and August, when water levels are down.

FLIES: Attractors, attractors, attractors. Later in the summer, consider terrestrial patterns like ants and beetles. Under bigger log jams, don't be afraid to swing a small, weighted Woolly Bugger.

OTHER NOTABLE YELLOWSTONE CUTTHROAT TROUT DESTINATIONS

TROUT LAKE is just north of the Northeast Entrance Road, west of the Northeast Entrance to the park. It's a short, uphill hike to the lake from the signed trailhead. No fishing is allowed at the inlet stream to protect spawners. Say hi to the family of otters that live there and that love to be photographed.

MCBRIDE LAKE empties into Slough Creek near the bottom end of Second Meadow. It's home to Yellowstone cutthroat trout that cruise the narrow lake. It's fun to find cruising fish and sight-cast to them.

PEBBLE CREEK flows into Soda Butte Creek and can be accessed from the campground on the north side of the Northeast Entrance Road. It doesn't look like much in the campground, as it flows almost due south to Soda Butte Creek, but it is home to small cutthroats. Higher up, about two or three miles or so, the fish get bigger. Foot-long cutthroats aren't uncommon as you work higher in to Pebble's meadow reaches. This is grizzly country. Be smart.

CACHE CREEK flows into the the Lamar River shortly before the latter meets Soda Butte Creek near the Northeast Entrance Road southeast of Silver Gate. This area was torched by the fires in 1988, but thanks to its connectivity with the Lamar and Yellowstone drainages, it has bounced back nicely. You'll find foot-long cutthroats here.

CASCADE LAKE is northwest of Canyon. It's an easy hike from the marked trailhead along the Grand Loop Road.

CASCADE CREEK flows out of Cascade Lake, runs east for a short bit and then turns south–southeast, running under the Norris-Canyon Road and eventually to the Yellowstone River, where it flows in between the upper and lower Yellowstone Falls. Its upper reaches can be accessed from the same trail to Cascade Lake. Its lower reaches are best accessed from the Cascade Trailhead west of Canyon.

BROAD CREEK is accessed from trailhead on the east side of the Yellowstone River, southeast of Canyon and north of Fishing Bridge. The

A bison lounges in the early summer grass near Cascade Creek, west of Canyon. *Photo by Chris Hunt.*

hike is about fourteen miles, but the fishing for cutthroats can be quite good. This isn't suitable for a day trip, but if you like to camp in the backcountry, this trip is a winner.

CUB CREEK, reached via the Thorofare Trail east of Yellowstone Lake, has a good population of fish but doesn't open until August 11 each summer. Chances of any big spawners still being in the creek when it opens? Minimal.

CLEAR CREEK is reached via the same Thorofare Trail as Cub Creek. It shares the same opening date, and by the time you get to fish it, most, if not all, of the big cutthroats will be back in Yellowstone Lake. You might get into spunky smaller cutthroats, however.

PELICAN CREEK is another Yellowstone Lake tributary. While most of the spawning cutthroats that use Pelican Creek will be long gone by the time it opens to anglers on July 15, it's still worth fishing for the odd straggler and the stream's resident fish, which likely use the creek for a year or so before migrating downstream to become lake fish, like their parents. It's a gorgeous meadow stream with beautiful meanders. You may only catch eight-inch cutthroats (or you might fool an eighteen-inch late-running cutty), but you'll be catching some stunning fish.

BEAVERDAM CREEK is accessed via the Thorofare Trailhead on the east side of Yellowstone Lake, just south of the East Entrance Road. It's a haul—probably more than ten miles. Honestly, I'd rent a boat from the marina and access Beaverdam Creek via the lake before I tried to hike in.

CHIPMUNK, GROUSE AND TRAIL CREEKS are found flowing into Yellowstone Lake in the South Arm and Southeast Arm. They can be reached via the Thorofare Trail that connects to the Trail Creek Trail, but it's a haul. Considering that most of the spawning trout in these creeks will be back in the lake by the time fishing opens on July 15, you might consider trying to reach these streams by boat.

HELLROARING CREEK flows south into Yellowstone National Park from Montana. It can be accessed east of Mammoth on the Grand Loop Road on a two-mile trail that goes straight down, and you'll have to wade across the Yellowstone River to reach the stream. The lower stretch of Hellroaring Creek is fishable and contains mid-sized cutthroats. Honestly, though, its best stretches for anglers are in Montana, before it enters Yellowstone. Remember, if you hike down, you'll have to hike up. Make sure you can make it back to the car.

SPORTSMAN'S LAKE is a small lake just inside the park boundary almost due west of Mammoth. It can be reached via a fifteen-mile hike that starts at the Glen Creek Trailhead between Mammoth and Norris, or from the east, via the Specimen and Fawn Pass Trailheads. Either way, this isn't a day hike, and it's not for the faint of heart. The fish, though, are true trophies. Cutthroats well over twenty inches can be caught here.

5

Snake River Fine-Spotted Cutthroat Trout

I have a dear friend—probably my best fishing buddy—who claims that I'm of the stubborn lot...that I just don't listen to her (and I should, she says, because she's always right).

The truth? Well, I'm guilty. Sometimes, I just have to find out for myself.

Years ago, another fishing buddy of mine told me that Crawfish Creek, just north of the south entrance to Yellowstone National Park, was fishless because its waters were poisoned by chemicals that leach out of a hot spring maybe a quarter of a mile from where the creek runs under South Entrance Road.

I've driven across Crawfish Creek a hundred times if I've driven over it once, and I've stopped to check out the creek's famous Moose Falls just downstream from the highway bridge, which is an impassable fish barrier for trout that might move up from the Lewis River.

Poison? The water looks clean and clear...and really fishy. It always has. There's some great pocket water, and it's full of woody debris that creates ideal trout habitat and some deep holes that just look like they'd hold big fish. I couldn't imagine that it was tainted by the likes of sulfur or other bowels-of-the-earth discharges that might kill fish. And it's named Crawfish Creek, for crying out loud. The name implies that it does, indeed, support life.

So, I found out for myself. And the answer is, we were both right.

From where Crawfish Creek crosses under the South Entrance Road to the confluence with tiny Spirea Creek, Crawfish Creek is really two streams. On the north side of the creek, the water is cold and clean. And

Lower Crawfish Creek, just above Moose Falls in the southern reaches of Yellowstone National Park. *Photo by Chris Hunt.*

it's fishy—after just a few casts of an attractor dry the first time I fished it, I managed to bring a couple of really pretty—and presumably native—cutthroat trout to hand. Nothing huge, but fat and healthy ten-inch cutties.

But when I crossed the creek to the south side, I noticed something different. The water was downright warm. And, yes, there were crawfish. Lots of them.

And the creek is only about thirty feet wide.

As I made my way upstream, I eventually came to Spirea Creek, which is the source of the cold, clean water. Crawfish Creek continues up into the timber, flowing generally west–northwest, and its waters are definitely influenced by hot springs inflows (although I'd be skeptical if it were actually "poisoned"). Spirea Creek, however, comes in from the north and generally flows north to south—it actually parallels the South Entrance Road for a while, but it's far enough away from the blacktop that motorists can't see it (and, thankfully, anglers can't see the motorists).

I ventured up Spirea Creek and spent a really fun afternoon catching Snake River fine-spotted cutthroat trout and larger-spotted, genetically identical Yellowstone cutthroats on small dry flies. It was one of those days where you lose track of time because the fishing is good and the wallpaper is simply stunning.

Spirea flows through a timbered meadow and features deep meanders and tight runs that require accurate casts, so it kept me entertained. And the fish were typical cutthroats—not at all shy, feisty and not terribly particular. If I remember correctly, I started and finished the day casting a size 16 Adams.

As the sun dipped behind the tops of the lodgepoles on the west side of the creek and the summer air cooled as evening got closer, the mosquitoes started to come out in earnest. Time to go.

Rather than retrace my steps and venture back down Crawfish Creek, I took my bearings and simply bushwhacked back to the South Entrance Road—maybe a third of a mile. From there, I walked south down the pavement to where I'd parked my rig, just north of the bridge above Moose Falls.

That's how you kill an afternoon in Yellowstone. And, to my fishing buddy who's always right…hmph.

THE FISH

As noted in the previous chapter, the Snake River strain of cutthroat trout is virtually genetically identical to Yellowstone cutthroat trout, and biologists have struggled for years to determine if they are, indeed, a truly separate subspecies of cutthroat trout.

I'll leave that determination to the scientists who can take the deep genetic dive. For my purposes, I separated these trout from their Yellowstone siblings, simply because they inhabit streams on the western side of the Continental Divide, in the headwaters of the Snake River.

The Snake, of course, begins in Yellowstone's southern reaches, with some tributaries actually beginning in Wyoming's Bridger-Teton National Forest, and others running off the slopes of Two Ocean Plateau. The Snake winds its way through southern Yellowstone before leaving the park shortly after being joined by the Lewis River. Starting here, it flows generally south along the John D. Rockefeller Memorial Parkway, which separates Yellowstone from Grand Teton National Park.

While the Lewis River was most certainly a cutthroat stream prior to nonnative trout introductions in the once-fishless Lewis and Shoshone Lakes, it's now inhabited by browns and possibly lake trout that have spilled over the thirty-foot-tall Lewis Falls. The Snake, for whatever reason, continues to be a cutthroat trout stronghold, both above its confluence with the Lewis River and continuing south along the Rockefeller Parkway into Grand Teton National Park, where it eventually empties into Jackson Lake.

Sadly, the farther you go into the backcountry of Cascade Corner, the fewer cutthroats there seem to be. Native fish are just as often hybridized with nonnative rainbows that were planted generations ago in the Fall and Bechler Rivers, and, I would suspect, these fish have had some human help getting over the many waterfalls that might have otherwise kept the region's native trout intact. There are a few places where anglers can find native cutthroats in the southwest corner of the park, but as time passes, more hybridization takes place, and opportunities to catch native cutthroats diminish.

THE BEST PLACES TO CATCH SNAKE RIVER FINE-SPOTTED CUTTHROAT TROUT

The Snake River

Above the confluence with the Lewis River, the Snake remains one of the best cutthroat trout destinations in the southwest corner of the park. From where the Snake picks up the Heart River some fifteen miles upstream from where it leaves the park at the South Entrance, the stream is fairly easy to navigate, easy to fish and populated by eager native trout (and whitefish) willing to hit dry flies. Above the Heart River confluence, the Snake is a faster, higher-gradient, pocket-water and canyon stream that's full of smaller cutthroats. Anglers can reach this upper stretch by starting out along the South Boundary Trail for about eight miles to the Snake River Trail. This

OPPOSITE: Fall on the Snake River. *Photo by Chris Hunt.*

will take you many more miles into the backcountry for some great fishing for small cutthroats.

FLIES: Early in the year, after runoff has cleared a bit, consider going with small golden stonefly imitations, like the Yellow Sally, or mayfly imitations like a Green Drake in size 14 or so. As summer progresses and water levels subside, start using small terrestrials—ant and beetle patterns tied with foam and bright Antron can be deadly for rising cutthroats in the eight- to twelve-inch range. In the early fall, on cloudy days, switch over to Blue-winged Olives—these baetis mayfly imitations in size 18 to 20 can be absolutely deadly for fish gorging themselves before winter.

The Heart River

The Heart River flows out of Heart Lake several miles into the backcountry just off the Snake River Trail. The river doesn't open until July 1 due to frequent bear activity, and, honestly, it's likely not terribly accessible until then anyway—this corner of the park is the wettest part of Yellowstone, and it gets several feet of snow every winter. The lower part of the Heart River is a meandering meadow stream, and it's absolutely gorgeous. Higher up, it goes through a subtle canyon, which is mostly pocket water. The final mile or so of the Heart River—it's only four miles long once it leaves Heart Lake—is not as steep, and it's a great place to sight-cast to rising cutthroats in the twelve-to-sixteen-inch range. This is not a day trip—the hike to the lower end of the Heart River along the South Boundary Trail and the Snake River Trail is almost fifteen miles.

FLIES: Attractor dry flies should be your first option. If you like to nymph or drift nymphs under high-floating dries, the lower section of the Heart is ideal. I'd start with a greased-up Stimulator and maybe drop a size 14 Prince nymph about eighteen inches under it. If nymphing isn't your thing, you'll still have plenty of success with attractor dries on top.

Wolverine Creek

Wolverine Creek joins the Snake River along the South Boundary Trail just east of the Snake River Trail. Only a short stretch of Wolverine

Creek is actually in Yellowstone—most of Wolverine Creek and all of its tributaries, except for Harebell Creek, are in Wyoming's Bridger-Teton National Forest. (You'll need a Wyoming fishing license to fish that stretch of the creek.) But the short section in the park, maybe a third of a mile or so, is a productive cutthroat trout stream, with the native trout averaging about ten inches or so. It's worth a visit if you can do a ten-mile hike along the South Boundary Trail. Walk in early and plan to leave in time to get out before dark unless you get a backcountry camping permit. Of note: This is serious bear country. Don't go in without a can of bear spray, and make lots of noise while hiking.

FLIES: Again, it's simple. These fish don't see a lot of flies. Start with the attractors you like and go from there. Later in the summer, go with terrestrials—small ants and beetles will keep you entertained all day.

Heart Lake

Best accessed via the eight-mile-long Heart Lake Trail, Heart Lake is home to trophy cutthroat trout and introduced lake trout. (Anglers are required to kill any lake trout they catch.) It's the fourth-largest lake in the park, and it offers good fishing for cutthroats approaching twenty inches in length. (Lakers can be even bigger.) If you're in good shape and can handle the weight on the long hike, it's a great spot for a float tube.

FLIES: Go with streamers. Start with dark colors—black, brown and olive. Try 'Buggers and Slumpbusters to start, and they ought to be weighted, or fished on sink-tip lines. There can be sporadic mayfly and caddis hatches on the lake, so don't leave home without both imitations.

OTHER NOTABLE SNAKE RIVER FINE-SPOTTED CUTTHROAT TROUT DESTINATIONS

BEAVER CREEK flows into the northeast corner of Heart Lake. It's a spawning stream for Heart Lake's cutthroat trout, which will likely be back in the lake by mid-July. It's a long hike—probably close to ten miles along the Heart Lake Trail. This isn't for the day-tripper.

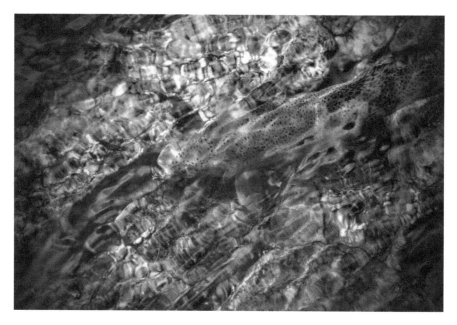

A Snake River fine-spotted cutthroat trout from the lower Lewis River, Yellowstone National Park. *Photo by Chris Hunt.*

OUTLET CREEK joins the Heart River just below the outlet from Heart Lake. It's a solid cutthroat stream boasting mid-sized trout, but it's a haul. Like Beaver Creek, this is best reserved for a multiple-night backcountry camping trip.

CRAWFISH CREEK and **SPIREA CREEK** are two easy-to-reach cutthroat streams that offer a backcountry feel while only being a short distance away from the road. Crawfish Creek flows under the South Entrance Road not too far north of the park's South Entrance. Crawfish Creek is thermally influenced, but its lower quarter mile or so is plenty fishy. Spirea Creek enters Crawfish Creek a quarter-mile upstream from the highway and is a great little trout stream.

The **LEWIS RIVER**, below Lewis Falls, has some cutthroats, but they share this river with brown trout. The best place to catch cutthroats in the Lewis River is downstream near its confluence with the Snake River.

MOUNTAIN ASH CREEK is west of the Southeast Entrance Road and is probably best reached using Reclamation Road out of Flagg Ranch, which is located outside Yellowstone's boundaries. You take Fish Lake Road north to its end. From there, it's a two-and-a-half-mile hike to Mountain Ash Creek. There are cutthroats here, but there are also rainbows and rainbow-cutthroat hybrids.

ROBINSON CREEK is one of the few fishing locations—in fact, it may be the only fishing location—in Yellowstone National Park that is located almost entirely in the skinny little stretch of Yellowstone that is in Idaho. (Its very upper reaches are in Wyoming.) The best place to get to Robinson Creek in the park is to bushwhack from Horseshoe Lake on the Targhee National Forest northeast of the community of Ashton. Use caution, though. The hike isn't marked by trails, and Robinson Creek lies in a steep canyon. There are cutthroats here, but there are also rainbows and rainbow-cutthroat hybrids, browns, brook trout and mountain whitefish.

6

Arctic Grayling

Cameron was just over a year old when he took his first steps in the cobble along the south shoreline of Grebe Lake in Yellowstone National Park.

My wife and I had hauled our little family down the three-and-a-half-mile trail from the Grebe Lake Trailhead between Norris and Canyon to the shores of this beautiful little backcountry lake for one simple reason.

I wanted to catch Arctic grayling.

Our daughter, Delaney, was not quite five, and she made the hike in without much trouble. It's not a tough walk, mostly flat through dead standing timber that burned in 1988. She toted a little pink Barbie backpack full of apple juice and string cheese—the perfect backcountry snack for a kindergartner. Cameron, on the other hand, made the journey in the "baby backpack" on his mom's shoulders, and from what I can remember, he slept most of the way.

I toted a larger pack with fishing gear, snacks, drinks and the like. For a day trip, we probably overdid it. But that's what parents do, I guess.

We arrived on the shores of Grebe Lake, relieved to shed our burdens. My wife spread out a little blanket not far from the water's edge, and I got busy assembling a 4-weight fly rod.

I'd caught grayling before, but here in the Intermountain West, their persistence largely depended on state fish and game agencies—native grayling hung on in a few places, like Montana's Big Hole River and a few other more remote waters. But in Yellowstone, where they were once abundant in the Gibbon, lower Firehole, Madison and Gallatin Rivers, they

were all but gone. In Grebe Lake, the native grayling that used to winter in the lake and then migrate into the inlet and outlet streams for the summer were, indeed, extirpated, largely thanks to the introduction of nonnative fish, like rainbow trout. The grayling that lived in Grebe were introduced by fisheries managers and were not native to the park. They were "adfluvial," meaning the vast majority of their life cycle was spent in lakes, not in rivers and streams.

It was a beautiful early summer day that blessed Yellowstone after winter's last gasp, which usually comes in late May. The trail into Grebe was clear of snow, but a few patches of winter clung to the north sides of big boulders. I dunked a toe into the lake. It was cold, as it should have been, but not numbingly so.

I tied on a small, size 10 olive Woolly Bugger and waded out into the lake up to my thighs and began casting my streamer over a noticeable drop-off. It didn't take long before I was hooked up. And the fish felt big.

Thrilled at the tug from the big fish, I let it run and take line from the reel, thinking that not only was I catching a grayling, but also a sizeable one. This, I thought, is about as good as it gets…standing miles away from the blacktop in the chilled waters of a wilderness lake connected to something wild.

A few minutes later, I landed a handsome seventeen-inch rainbow trout. I'd never in my life been disappointed in a fat-and-happy, football-shaped trout that fought like a freight train. Until that moment.

Where were the grayling?

Thankfully, I didn't have to wait long. A few casts later, and I managed to connect with a nice foot-long, sail-finned grayling that glistened under the summer sun. It was just gorgeous.

I fished for an hour or so and then wandered back to where Delaney was busy combing through the lakeside cobble, running her fingers over chunks of glass-like obsidian, and where my wife and Cameron were walking along the bank, putting their toes in and out of the lake's clear water. I watched as his mom let go of one hand, and then the other, and marveled as my son took his very first steps before plopping down unceremoniously on his butt.

OPPOSITE: Arctic grayling from Cascade Lake, Yellowstone National Park. *Photo by Chris Hunt.*

The cheers from his mom and dad brought a big smile to his face, and that's a grin I'll never forget.

Shortly after we plowed through the snacks and the juice and the water, we loaded everything back into the backpack and began the hike back to the car, and back to civilization. Delaney dutifully donned her Barbie pack, my wife toted the now-walkable boy and I put everything else in my backpack. About a mile back to the car, Delaney begged for a rest.

"Will you carry me, Daddy?" she asked. I reached down, picked her up and slung her to my shoulders.

"You're getting so big!" I exclaimed. She put her hands on top of my head, like she always did, and enjoyed the ride. It lasted for another mile, and I was spent.

"Honey," I said. "You're going to have to walk. I can't carry you anymore."

"It's OK, Daddy," she said. "I'm not tired anymore." I plopped her down, and she started up the trail like a trooper.

We got back to the car about half an hour later and started putting all the gear away. I tucked my backpack and all my fishing gear into the back of the vehicle and then reached down and grabbed Delaney's little pink pack. It was heavy. Way too heavy.

I opened it up and found it full of glistening black obsidian, or larger igneous stones that contained hunks of the volcanic glass. There were dozens of them. No wonder she felt so heavy when I put her on my shoulders. The kid walked out of Grebe Lake with a Barbie backpack bursting with rocks.

And, of course, removing geologic and archaeologic items from the national park is illegal, so I had to explain to my devastated little girl why she couldn't take these beautiful rocks home. The tears were unbearable.

It's a funny story her mom and I still tell to this day—how she managed to wander out of Grebe Lake with twenty pounds of stones in her backpack, I'll never know. But we dutifully spread the rocks around on the ground near the trailhead and explained to our little girl that she wasn't to take anything from the park ever again.

That was probably fifteen years ago. Cameron is now driving, and Delaney is out on her own having her own adventures. She'll never forget Grebe Lake, and neither will I. Or the grayling that brought us there.

THE FISH

W.C. Kendall, the assistant with the U.S. Bureau of Fisheries in 1914, had this to say about Yellowstone's native grayling in *The Fishes of Yellowstone National Park*:

The Montana grayling originally existed only in tributaries of the Missouri River above Great Falls.

In the park it occurs naturally in Madison and Gallatin Rivers and branches, Fan Creek, Grayling Creek, and the Firehole River below the falls. It is reported as very abundant at the junction of Firehole and Gibbon Rivers. It is said to ascend, in summer, as far as Firehole Falls and to be found in the Gallatin River in the northwestern part of the park.

The Montana grayling is a most graceful and beautiful fish, of shapely proportions and exquisite coloration. The adult averages from 10 to 12 inches in length and...to 1 pound in weight.

It prefers swift, clear, pure streams, with gravelly or sandy bottom. It is quite gregarious, lying in schools in the deeper pools, in plain sight, and not, like the trout, concealed under bushes and overhanging banks. In search of food, which consists principally of bisects and their larvae, it occasionally extends its range to streams strewn with bowlders [sic] and broken rocks.

Unlike the native trout, the grayling will go long distances, if necessary, to find suitable spawning grounds. They spawn in April and May on gravelly shallows. In the north fork of the Madison River, where the water is comparatively warm, coming from the Firehole River in the Yellowstone Park, the grayling spawns a month earlier than in any other waters in Montana.

In point of activity it even excels the native trout, when hooked breaking the water repeatedly in its effort to escape, which the trout seldom does. It takes the artificial fly eagerly, and if missed at the first cast will rise again and again from the depths of the pool, whereas the trout will seldom rise a second time without a rest. It will also take various baits, such as caddis-fly larvae, grasshoppers, and worms. Among the recommended flies are professor, Lord Baltimore, queen of the water, grizzly king, Henshall, coachman, and various gauze-winged flies, with no. 10 and 12 hooks.

As a food fish it is even better than the trout. Its flesh is firm and flaky, very white, and of delicate flavor.

Grayling are truly special and, sadly, all but lost to their native waters in Montana and Wyoming. Before European Americans pioneered the West, these beautiful salmonids were native throughout the upper Missouri River drainage. They were documented by the Lewis and Clark expedition in the Missouri River as "a new kind of white or silvery trout."

Every time I remember that they were once plentiful, I'm blown away by how, in just over a century, they've all but disappeared from the Lower 48. The population in the headwaters of the Missouri is on the ropes. A population native to Michigan is extinct (but restoration efforts are underway). Of course, after reading Kendall's account about how naive and easily caught the fish were one hundred years ago, I guess it shouldn't come as a surprise. As we've tamed the West with irrigation canals and let cattle roam along our rivers and streams and generally changed the landscape and the watersheds to suit our needs, the loss of the fragile grayling is but one of many ecological tragedies.

Today, they cling to existence in the upper reaches of the Big Hole River and in a few other places where they've been targeted for restoration in Montana. Results have been mixed. In Yellowstone, the grayling that once plied the waters of the Gallatin River's main stem were gone by 1900, according to a 2017 article in *Yellowstone Science* written by Koel, Jeff L. Arnold, Colleen R. Detjens, Brian D. Ertel and Michael E. Ruhl, and they were gone completely in the park by 1935.

In Yellowstone, past efforts to bring native, fluvial grayling back to their home waters have all failed, and that's largely because, of all the park's native salmonids, grayling do not compete well with nonnative trout. Browns, rainbows and brook trout have taken over native grayling waters in the park.

But the tide might be turning.

As noted in Yellowstone's Native Fish Conservation Plan, there is a concerted effort to restore native fish to their historic waters. And grayling, along with the west slope cutthroat trout that the grayling evolved alongside (and was also all but extinct from Yellowstone's waters), are atop the list. Today, there are several projects ongoing to return grayling to Yellowstone, where anglers will be one of the primary beneficiaries.

The very same Grebe Lake where my son took his first steps lies atop the Gibbon River drainage, and it, along with Wolf Lake and the Gibbon River above little Gibbon Falls (located just north of the Norris-Canyon Road), have been "treated" with piscicides to remove nonnative adfluvial grayling, rainbow trout and brook trout. The first treatment was in the summer of 2017, with a subsequent treatment in 2018. (The latter treatment was in the river between Little Gibbon Falls and Virginia Cascades—Grebe and Wolf Lakes were just treated once.) Native west slope cutthroat trout—descendants of a brood-stock found several years back in a tiny, remote stream on the park's western fringes—and native fluvial grayling have been introduced.

In the summer of 2018, I was in Jacklin's Fly Shop in West Yellowstone and overheard a customer talking about how he actually caught grayling in the upper Gibbon above Virginia Cascades (which means the fish are spreading, because Virginia Cascades is below Little Gibbon Falls). I was, to say the least, thrilled.

Another ongoing project is on Grayling Creek, which is located north of West Yellowstone. Grayling Creek is a tributary to the Madison River, via Hebgen Reservoir. The National Park Service has enhanced a natural waterfall to make it a complete fish barrier on Grayling Creek to keep nonnative browns and rainbows from the reservoir from running up the creek. After treating the upper reaches of Grayling Creek, native west slope cutthroat trout and grayling are swimming once again in their native waters.

THE BEST PLACES TO CATCH GRAYLING IN YELLOWSTONE NATIONAL PARK

Grayling Creek

Grayling Creek is located a short drive north of West Yellowstone and is one of the restoration sites for native fluvial Arctic grayling. The stream is easily accessed by roadside anglers and actually offers a pretty good chance to catch these rare native fish. The stream is a typical high-country freestone creek that offers good structure and cover, nice, deep runs, some meadow stretches and easy-to-read water. It's also home to native west slope cutthroat trout, which are being restored alongside the native grayling. (Both fish have been reintroduced above a waterfall the park service improved to serve as a barrier to prevent nonnative trout migrating upstream from Hebgen Lake.) The fish, only a few years into the restoration effort, aren't huge. A foot-long grayling would be a trophy.

FLIES: Attractor dries should be your first choice—consider a Royal Coachman or a Royal Wulff Trude or something that floats high and is easily visible by you. Grayling have smaller mouths than trout, so don't go too big—no matter what dry fly you pick, don't go much bigger than a size 14. Another good option would be to go with a size 14 Stimulator and drop a size 16 Prince Nymph about a foot under it.

Grebe Lake

While the fish in Grebe Lake are now "fluvial," thanks to recent restoration and reintroduction efforts, there are still fish—and will be in the coming years—that are worth chasing. The three-and-a-half-mile hike in from the Grebe Lake Trailhead on the north side of the Norris Canyon Road is pretty easy—hearty anglers might even consider toting a float tube into the backcountry to get to deeper water, where the resident fish will be later in the summer. These fish were only recently reintroduced. They won't be sizeable for another year or two, but Grebe Lake is gorgeous. It's worth the short hike.

FLIES: Small streamers should work. Later in the summer, you'll need to go deep, so consider a sinking or sink-tip line. A size 10–12 bead-head Woolly Bugger in olive or black would be my first choice. In the evenings, watch for rising fish. Grayling will feed on the top in lakes. Also, don't shy away from stripping some larger nymphs, like Hare's-Ear, Copper Johns, Princes and the like.

Wolf Lake

Wolf Lake is part of Yellowstone's grayling and west slope cutthroat trout restoration effort, just like Grebe Lake. It's lower down in the drainage and connected to Grebe Lake by the Gibbon River (which is a really small stream as it runs between the two lakes). Wolf Lake is quite a bit smaller than Grebe Lake. The quickest way to get to Wolf Lake is actually via the Grebe Lake Trail, but you can also access it from the Wolf Lake Trail, which starts on the north side of the Norris-Canyon Road and follows the upper Gibbon River for a short distance before cutting across country and taking a more direct route to Wolf Lake. It's a longer hike, but you can fish the upper Gibbon on the way.

FLIES: Just like with Grebe Lake, start with small streamers ('Buggers, Zonkers, Slumpbusters, etc.). Don't be afraid to slowly strip large nymphs you might only consider for moving water—in nearby Cascade Lake, where there remains a population of nonnative adfluvial grayling, a bead-head Hare's-Ear nymph in olive or a rusty brown seems to really get the fish's attention.

Cascade Lake

Cascade Lake is reached via a short and easy hike from the Cascade Lake Trailhead on the Grand Loop Road north of Canyon. It crosses over Cascade Creek, which is home to native Yellowstone cutthroat trout. The lake, though, is home to both cutthroats and an introduced population of adfluvial (lake-dwelling) grayling. I've fished this lake a few times and, subsequently, Cascade Creek, and I've never seen a grayling in the creek itself (but I have caught them near the outlet). It's a small lake, and it's a popular hike, but, oddly, not a lot of hikers tote fishing gear with them. The fishing can be really good for grayling and the native cutthroats.

Hiking the Cascade Lake Trail in search of cutthroats and grayling. *Photo by Chris Hunt.*

FLIES: Small streamers—'Buggers, Slumpbusters, Zonkers, Muddlers, etc.—should be your first choice. If they don't work, go smaller—use nymphs you might otherwise only use for fishing rivers and streams, and slowly retrieve them. Parts of the shoreline have weed beds—strip flies next to this structure. You'll be glad you did. Flies weighted with bead-heads will work best.

Upper Gibbon River

The Gibbon River heads in Grebe Lake about three and a half miles north of the Norris Canyon Road between Norris Junction and Canyon. It flows southwest into Wolf Lake and then southwest where it picks up the drainage from the Norris Geyser Basin and a host of hot springs and hot pools before plunging over Gibbon Falls and eventually meeting up with the Firehole River. This wedding of these two rivers creates the fabled Madison.

In the upper Gibbon River, above the natural fish barrier that is Virginia Cascade, the Gibbon is once again home to native, fluvial (migrating between lakes and rivers) Arctic grayling. Starting in 2017 and continuing in 2018, the National Park Service removed nonnative rainbow and brook trout and introduced adfluvial (lake-dwelling) grayling from drainage, starting with Grebe Lake all the way down to Virginia Cascade. Native grayling were reintroduced in 2017, and a second planting was done in 2018 (along with native west slope cutthroat trout). To get to the easiest-accessible stretch of the Gibbon, take the side road to Virginia Cascade between Norris Junction and Canyon, and drive up above the big, beautiful waterfall. Another great access point is the Wolf Lake Trail, which follows the upper Gibbon to Little Gibbon Falls, a second fish barrier that protects the newly reintroduced native fish from nonnative fish all the way to the headwaters, just in case the piscicide treatments lower downstream prove unsuccessful.

OPPOSITE: Craig Copeland of New South Wales, Australia, casts for trout in the upper Gibbon River. This stretch of river is now home to restored populations of grayling and west slope cutthroat trout.

FLIES: There's absolutely no reason to get fancy here. I'd start with something easy to see—say, a size 12 to 14 Adams—and I might not change flies all day. Later in the summer, switch to small terrestrials. Hoppers, ants and beetles should be money in late July through early September. Honestly, though, any attractor pattern should do the trick. In the off chance that the grayling aren't looking up, consider dropping a small nymph—again, the pattern probably isn't important—about sixteen inches under your dry fly.

7

Rainbow Trout

t was probably close to twenty years ago when I heard legendary angler Jack Dennis talk about the bright and aggressive rainbow trout in the Fall River at the Eastern Idaho Fly Tying Expo in Idaho Falls.

I was new to the area, having just moved to Pocatello from northern California to take a job as a newspaper editor. I spent two days at the expo, gathering all the intel I could on local waters—I had a lot to learn about the region's fisheries. I figured this annual gathering was the best place to start.

I filled up two notebooks that weekend and drove to Idaho Falls and back to Pocatello three times, much to the chagrin of my wife, who, I'm sure, wondered what became of her husband for the better part of two days during a blustery weekend in April. That weekend was the genesis of all my Yellowstone fishing adventures, even though I'd yet to set foot in the park with a fly rod in hand. I just remember Jack working a slide projector in a dark meeting room at the Shilo Inn, transporting me to the park's southwest corner and the Fall River that, to this day, I believe to be one of the most beautiful trout streams on the planet.

He clicked through the slides and stopped at a gorgeous scene of maybe the perfect waterfall. It stretched the width of the river and had to have been the most naturally uniform cascade ever crafted by the forces of nature. Cave Falls isn't a massive waterfall—it's only 20 feet tall. But it's more than 250 feet wide, and tucked along the river's northwest shoreline was a subtle cave that gives the waterfall its name.

A typical Madison River rainbow trout. *Photo by Chris Hunt.*

"I've stood right there," Jack said, pointing a laser at the screen, at just about the base of the little cave, "and cast a Royal Wulff right into the cave and caught fish."

Nobody can duplicate that feat again, and it's not because the cast was terribly difficult. Sadly, just a few years ago, the cave that gave the waterfall its name collapsed. Erosion and the constant subtle shaking that Yellowstone endures on a daily basis—the park experiences anywhere between one thousand and three thousand earthquakes a year, most so small they can't be felt—finally took a toll on the overhanging rock.

But Jack was right about one thing. The Fall River's rainbows are tailwalkers, and they are bright and beautiful and wonderfully optimistic, if a bit on the small size. And my favorite place to fish is directly below Cave Falls, so close to the waterfall that my sunglasses mist over. In the heavy chop and along the seams, ten- to twelve-inch rainbows will launch themselves after dry flies. Bigger fish—a trophy in this stretch would be a fat fifteen-incher—will chase streamers on the swing.

But, in recent years, I've learned that the best way to chase the Fall River's rainbows is with small soft-hackles dead-drifted through the chop and then allowed to swing out below me. This method is downright deadly.

This is also usually one of the first places in the park I'll visit in the spring. While the water will run high, it almost never runs dirty. Even on opening weekend the last Saturday in May, the Fall River is dependably clean. It's a great place to wash off winter, work out the kinks in an awakened fly cast and, most importantly, catch some beautiful wild rainbow trout.

THE FISH

The Kendall/Smith report claims that rainbows were first planted in Yellowstone National Park in Grebe Lake atop the Gibbon River drainage in 1889. The Varley report documents a 1909 stocking. The former report also intimates—but it's not certain—that the source for these nonnative trout was the McCloud River in California.

Rainbows are native to the West's coastal streams, and their inland kin, the redband trout, are native as far east as northwest Montana and central Idaho. But rainbows are not native to any Yellowstone watershed.

Unfortunately, rainbows and native cutthroat trout mix quite well on spawning redds in the spring. The resulting offspring are fertile hybrids many refer to simply as "cuttbows." Over time, as rainbows and the fertile hybrids continue to spawn and move into new habitat, they take over waters where native cutthroat trout evolved. All across the West, native cutthroat trout occupy only a small percentage of their native range, and a lot of the blame for that can be prescribed to the interloping rainbows and the fisheries managers generations ago who were more inclined to answer the call to spice up America's fisheries than they were to protect our native trout.

Rainbows not only wash away the genetic integrity of native cutthroats here in the West. They also are among the culprits that have relegated eastern brook trout in Appalachia to the small, headwater streams where they are native.

Considering all the bad things about rainbows, you might forgive me if I were to advocate the catch and kill of every rainbow I bring to hand. While I do kill my share of rainbows that turn up in cutthroat trout water, in Yellowstone, these exotic fish are no longer just visitors. They're part of the angling fabric of the park—they are part of Yellowstone's fishing heritage.

And, while the National Park Service is doing its best to restore native trout and grayling to their native watersheds, there will always be rainbow trout in Yellowstone for anglers to pursue. There'll always be rainbows in the Gibbon, the Madison and the Firehole.

And in the Fall River, too, of course. For that, I'm grateful.

BEST PLACES TO CATCH RAINBOW TROUT IN YELLOWSTONE NATIONAL PARK

The Madison River

Resident rainbows in the Madison River within the park's boundaries are pretty hardy fish. The Madison in the park is formed where the Gibbon and the Firehole—both thermally influenced rivers—come together near Madison Junction. Even in normal years, when water temperatures don't get excessively warm, resident rainbow trout (and brown trout, for that matter) deal with water temperatures that regularly approach seventy degrees. During particularly hot summers, the National Park Service will often close the Madison to fishing.

But, early in the year, from opening weekend to about the first week of July, the Madison is a great place to catch rainbow trout on the fly. Access along the West Entrance Road is plentiful, and the river offers all kinds of great holding water, from winding meadow reaches near its headwaters, to long, fishy riffles in the river's lower third. Truly big rainbows enter the river in the fall as they follow big brown trout up from Hebgen Lake in Montana on the latter's spawning run.

OPPOSITE: Two young bull elk spar on the banks of the Madison River in preparation for more serious battles in the years to come. *Photo by Chris Hunt.*

FLIES: Early in the year, particularly if the park has received any spring moisture at all, consider going with a size 12 Green Drake. But, as early as the first or second week of June, the Madison sees a good salmonfly hatch, so don't hesitate to throw big bugs. Sizes 8 to 10 foam stonefly patterns will work surprisingly well, and it also might be the best time of the year, save for the fall spawning run of browns, to catch a big fish on the Madison in the park. Accordingly, don't shy away from using big stonefly nymphs—again, size 8 or so—under indicators or high-floating dry flies, like a big Chernobyl. In the fall, egg patterns are a good bet for rainbows that have followed the browns up out of Hebgen.

The Firehole River

Rainbows are present throughout the Firehole River system, from its headwaters well above Old Faithful all the way to its meeting with the

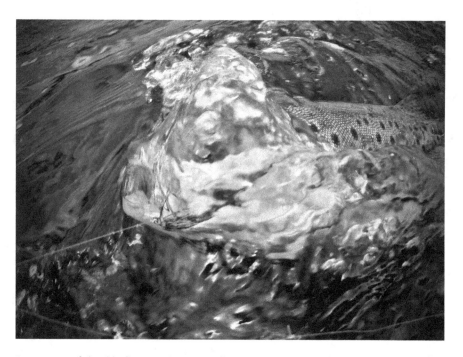

Swinging soft-hackle flies can be very effective on the Firehole, Gibbon and Madison Rivers. *Photo by Chris Hunt.*

Gibbon where it helps form the Madison. The Firehole fishes very well early in the season—it's one of my favorite "opening day" streams that I'll occasionally hit on the Saturday before Memorial Day in late May. As the weather warms and the thermal inflows to the Firehole team up with the hot weather, the fishing in the Firehole slows down significantly—many of the river's fish move up into cooler tributaries or hover over cold spring seeps to stay cool. The fishing in the Firehole picks up again in mid-September and fishes really well through October.

FLIES: Craig Mathews has converted me into a soft-hackle swinger, and the Firehole is the reason why. Yes, you can catch rainbows (and browns) on the Firehole using dry flies, nymphs and streamers—and all work well at certain times. But while fish will sip a dry fly or subtly suck in a nymph, they will *hammer* a soft-hackle on the swing just below the surface. Go with Blue-winged Olive and PMD soft-hackles, and cast them upstream and across the river through fishy runs. They'll float dry for a bit (particularly if you coat them in Gink), and you might get a strike when they do. But when the fly begins to swing, and it dips just under the surface…that's when the fun starts. Also, the Firehole is famous for its white miller caddis hatch. These awkward insects can be prolific, and the trout love them. Check out Blue Ribbon Flies in West Yellowstone for some great patterns imitating this funky bug.

The Gibbon River

Given that the Gibbon is the first place in the park to receive rainbow trout, it makes sense that it's worth a shot if wild rainbows are on your wish list. The lower Gibbon above its meeting with the Firehole can be particularly good for rainbows early in the season and again in September and October. Higher up, in Gibbon and Elk Meadows, brown trout rule the roost, so the lower reaches are really your best bet.

FLIES: Early in the year, there is a pretty solid stonefly hatch (usually in early June), so start with big nymphs (size 8 or so), and when you see naturals streamside, go with dry imitations. White miller caddis are prolific on the lower river, and during cooler summers, the lower Gibbon is a great place to fish terrestrials.

Gibbon Falls from above the lower Gibbon River.
Photo by Chris Hunt.

The Gallatin River

North of West Yellowstone, Montana, the Gallatin River flows north down the Gallatin Canyon toward Bozeman, Montana. In its headwaters in Yellowstone National Park, introduced rainbow trout are common and can be caught in a really pretty meadow setting. The river is easily accessed from U.S. Highway 191 via a number of pullouts, and it flows under the highway a couple of times as it meanders downstream toward its confluence with Specimen Creek. The Gallatin flows out of Gallatin Lake in the Yellowstone backcountry. This section of the river is accessed by the Bighorn Pass Trail that can be accessed off the highway just north of Divide Lake. Use caution—this is bear country. Have your bear spray with you.

FLIES: In the lower reaches below Specimen Creek, there is a good stonefly hatch that usually starts in late June or early July, depending on the weather. The river here is faster, too, and more of the freestone stream that you might remember from the footage shot in *A River Runs Through It* that was filmed on the Gallatin in the 1990s. Go with high-floating dries and drop a stonefly nymph under it in these reaches—if and when you see naturals on the water, go big. Higher up, in the meadow stretches, go with dry attractors to start. If nothing is happening, drop a nymph under your fly or under an indicator. Later in the summer, go with hoppers, ants and beetles—these terrestrials will draw aggressive strikes from rainbows.

The Bechler River

This is the best place in Yellowstone National Park to catch truly big rainbows. Planted sometime around the turn of the last century, the Bechler's rainbows are legendary—fish in the twenty-two-to-twenty-four-inch range aren't uncommon. The best way to the famous Bechler Meadows is via the trailhead at the Bechler Ranger Station situated in the far southwest corner of the park. From there, it's about three and a half miles to the meadows. You can also reach the meadows via the Cave Falls trail that closely follows the Bechler above its confluence with the Fall River. The fishing in the lower Bechler can be good, but the fish aren't nearly as big as the trophies that lurk in the meadows. Fall is the best time to visit the meadows—this corner of Yellowstone features a lot of standing water, and therefore, a lot of voracious mosquitoes. I hiked into the meadows once in mid-July. I'll never

do it again—and the fishing was good. I usually wait until September, when things dry out a bit, and the bugs have subsided.

FLIES: In the lower river's rapids and pocket water, attractor dries that both you and the fish can see should work well. If you plan to fish the meadows, bring your A game and be prepared to match the hatch and cast to fish that can be quite picky. Early in the year, PMDs will hatch almost every day, so don't leave home without a handful of imitations in the size 16 range. On blustery days early or late in the season, Blue-winged Olives will come in handy. Nymphing this stretch is a great way to catch big fish, and you'll need caddis imitations, bead-head Hare's-Ears, Pheasant Tails and the like. Later in the year, hoppers will cause some of the bigger fish to lose some of their inhibitions.

OTHER NOTABLE RAINBOW TROUT DESTINATIONS IN YELLOWSTONE NATIONAL PARK

The **FALL RIVER** above and below Cave Falls is a great place to catch feisty rainbows. The upper Fall River can be accessed at the Cascade Creek trailhead off of Reclamation Road, which is outside the park in Wyoming. It's a short hike to the river, which is more intimate in this reach and actually boasts some decent rainbows in the twelve-to-fourteen-inch range. It can also be accessed lower down, off of Fish Lake Road via the Fish Lake Trail. Finally, anglers can get to the upper reaches of the Fall River at the Grassy Lake Trailhead, also off of Reclamation Road.

    CASCADE CREEK flows north out of Lake of the Woods and under Reclamation Road before entering Yellowstone. It's home to some fun rainbows in the ten- to twelve-inch range before it flows into the Fall River. This is not the same Cascade Creek that flows in the Yellowstone River south of Canyon.

OPPOSITE, TOP: Rachel Andona casts to rainbows on the lower Bechler River. *Photo by Chris Hunt.*

OPPOSITE, BOTTOM: Cave Falls, Yellowstone National Park. *Photo by Chris Hunt.*

ROBINSON CREEK is home to rainbows, as well as cutthroats, cuttbows, browns, brookies and whitefish. It's best accessed via a bushwhack from Horseshoe Lake in Idaho. It's a beast of a hike down into a very deep canyon and an even worse hump coming out. But the fishing can be quite good.

BOUNDARY CREEK flows into the Bechler River just below Bechler Meadows. Rainbows here are big and picky, just like their relatives in the Bechler.

SLOUGH CREEK, mostly in the lower section, has an invading population of rainbows that apparently migrated up from the Lamar River or the Yellowstone River. None of this is good news for any of the aforementioned streams. Consider keeping your catch.

The **GARDNER RIVER** has a few rainbows in its lower reaches inside the park. They compete with brook trout higher up and brown trout in the more arid lower stretch.

8
West Slope Cutthroat Trout

Todd Koel, the lead fisheries biologist for Yellowstone, had walked a group of us through the lodgepoles just west of U.S. Highway 89, far into the northwest corner of Yellowstone National Park, to where we all stood on a bluff overlooking Grayling Creek, some ways down in the valley.

Near here, he explained to a group of fishing bloggers and Trout Unlimited staffers and volunteers, would be the weir—the National Park Service would "enhance" a natural waterfall that would serve as a fish barrier to keep brown and rainbow trout from nearby Hebgen Lake from migrating up Grayling Creek. Only with that weir, Koel explained, could native west slope cutthroat trout and Arctic grayling be reintroduced to this watershed—a native watershed—and stand a fighting chance.

That was July 2012. Since then, the weir has been constructed, and both native west slope cutthroat trout and Arctic grayling (the two species evolved alongside each other in the Missouri River drainage) have been reintroduced above that barrier. It's now a "fishable" population of native fish in the park.

On that same Trout Unlimited tour, we were treated to some of the more "hands-on" work the National Park Service is doing since it released the Native Fish Conservation Plan. Not only did we get to see the site of this future recovery project, but we also got to go out on gillnet and box-net boats and actually took an active role in removing nonnative lake trout from Yellowstone Lake.

We also helped a crew of biologists on a fish-shocking effort in upper Soda Butte Creek, where nonnative brook trout were showing up in that

A cow moose strides across a meadow near the Gibbon River. *Photo by Chris Hunt.*

stream, which is home to an important population of native Yellowstone cutthroat trout.

Also on that trip, we ventured up Slough Creek, which is of particular interest to the park service because nonnative rainbow trout were showing up in the creek's lower reaches, and because rainbows and cutthroats can mingle on spawning beds—the resulting offspring, often called "cutbows," are fertile hybrids. This discovery could threaten the genetic integrity of the native Yellowstone cutthroat trout that make Slough Creek the amazing dry fly-fishery that it is.

West slope cutthroat trout, though, were so close to the brink of extinction in Yellowstone that the park's fisheries biologists believed them to be completely gone by the 1930s. Only the discovery of two holdover populations in remote streams in 2005 made it possible for the native trout to begin a recovery. Today, there are several locations where native west slope cutthroat swim in Yellowstone—and the effort to improve their numbers and their populations will continue. In fact, in order to improve the chances of recovery and reduce the impacts to Yellowstone's west slope cutthroats from events like fires or floods that might wash out fish barriers, the Park Service has established a population of the fish in Goose Lake and a chain of connected small lakes in the upper Firehole drainage—these lakes were formerly fishless, and there's no aboveground connection between them and the upper Firehole, which is occupied by nonnative brown and rainbow trout.

This is good, thoughtful planning on the part of Koel and his team of fisheries biologists in the park. It shows just how serious the National Park Service is about recovering this native fish within Yellowstone. And it's great news for anglers who, in the near future, might have even more waters to visit in order to catch native west slope cutthroat trout.

THE FISH

Sometime in the 1920s, the National Park Service planted cutthroat trout in a tiny creek hidden in the Yellowstone River drainage, very likely not knowing that the progeny of those fish would one day help resuscitate Yellowstone National Park's native west slope cutthroat trout population.

Geode Creek flows into the Yellowstone River north of Canyon and is separated from the downstream population of native Yellowstone cutthroat trout by waterfalls. Why west slope cutthroats were transplanted to the Yellowstone drainage is anybody's guess, but it serves to demonstrate how little was known about the park's native trout, the genetic differences among them and the geographical ranges each subspecies occupied in the early part of the twentieth century. Sadly, by the 1930s, west slope cutthroat trout within the boundaries of Yellowstone National Park were thought to be extinct. So, the "happy accident" in Geode Creek is quite significant.

The west slope cutthroat population in Geode Creek was "discovered" in August 2005, which was a big year for these native fish. Earlier that summer, a small relict population of west slopes was found in what is now fittingly called Last Chance Creek, a very small tributary to Grayling Creek northwest of West Yellowstone, Montana.

Today, the progeny of these rediscovered trout are swimming in more of their native waters, and there are several fishable populations of west slope cutthroat trout within Yellowstone. This is good news, not only for anglers, but also the subspecies. West slope cutthroats and Yellowstone cutthroats likely evolved from a common ancestor, eons ago. Today, west slope cutthroat trout in the Missouri River drainage occupy only 5 percent of their native range. The "new" Yellowstone National Park populations give the subspecies a substantial boost.

THE BEST PLACES TO CATCH WEST SLOPE CUTTHROAT TROUT IN YELLOWSTONE NATIONAL PARK

High Lake

High Lake sits at 8,800 feet above sea level and is the source of the East Fork of Specimen Creek and was the first body of water in the park where native west slope cutthroat trout were reintroduced. Originally fishless, it was stocked with nonnative Yellowstone cutthroat trout in 1937, which meant, in order to start the west slope cutthroat recovery project, the seven-acre lake had to be treated first. It's separated from the downstream reaches of the East Fork of Specimen Creek by a waterfall, so, once treated, there was little threat of nonnative fish coming back to the lake. All the nonnative trout were removed from High Lake in 2006, and between 2007 and 2009, it was stocked with west slope cutthroat trout. Honestly, the effort to get to High Lake is likely not worth the reward, unless you absolutely love to hike and camp in the backcountry—it's at least a fifteen-mile hike using the Specimen Creek and Crescent Lake trail. It's definitely not a day trip.

FLIES: If you brave the hike, start with streamers. The lake isn't very big, but it drops off pretty quickly from the edges. I'd go with a weighted black Woolly Bugger or a weighted Muddler Minnow in a size 10 to start. In the evenings, dry flies might be an option—lakes in and around the park can sport prolific mayfly hatches once the sun dips behind the trees. I'd throw an Adams in a size 14.

East Fork Specimen Creek

The National Park Service completed a log fish barrier on the East Fork of Specimen Creek above its confluence with the North Fork of Specimen

Creek. The creek was treated several times with the piscicide rotenone from High Lake all the way down to the barrier, and, starting in 2010, about ten thousand "eyed" west slope cutthroat trout eggs were placed in remote-site incubators in the creek. As of the latest survey in 2016, the East Fork of Specimen Creek is now home to a healthy, naturally reproducing population of west slope cutthroat trout. Getting to the lower reaches of the East Fork of Specimen Creek is a breeze—it's a quick two-mile hike.

FLIES: When we toured the Specimen Creek area in 2013, we found lots of caddis flies under overturned rocks—their little pebble "houses" were everywhere, so it seems like these bugs would be a significant part of any trout's diet in this watershed. Consider caddis and caddis emergers, along with drifted nymphs. Later in the summer, go with a high-floating terrestrial pattern, like an ant or a beetle, and drop a caddis nymph about sixteen inches under your dry fly.

Grayling Creek

Just as with Yellowstone's reintroduced population of Arctic grayling, west slope cutthroats are benefiting from the improved waterfall on the lower reaches of Grayling Creek that is keeping nonnative browns and rainbows from Hebgen Lake out of their new home. Grayling Creek is easily accessed along U.S. Highway 191 north of West Yellowstone—it's a classic freestone mountain creek that features just about anything you might want in a trout stream. It has a gorgeous canyon stretch with great pocket water; beautiful meadow reaches with meanders, deep bends and long runs; and fast-water stretches through thick timber.

FLIES: Cutthroats (and grayling, for that matter) always seem to be looking up. I'd fish for the cuties the same way I'd fish for the grayling—a heavy dose of attractor dries to start. Later in summer, I'd put on a foam terrestrial, like a small hopper, ant or beetle, and drop a size 14 Prince Nymph under it.

Upper Gibbon River

Above Virginia Cascades, the Gibbon River is really just a small stream—maybe fifteen feet wide at most. For years, this was where I'd take my kids to catch very willing brook trout whenever we'd visit the park. However, in the 2010 Native Fish Conservation Plan, the upper Gibbon drainage, which includes Wolf, Grebe and Ice Lakes, was identified as a future site for a restored population of native west slope cutthroat trout and fluvial grayling. The drainage was treated in the summers of 2017 and 2018 to remove nonnative trout, and west slope cutthroats were stocked, along with Arctic grayling. The upper Gibbon is the picturesque Yellowstone stream, easily accessed from the Norris-Canyon Road or, even better, from the scenic drive to Virginia Cascade. Just before it falls sixty feet over a cliff, the Gibbon is a meandering meadow stream with deep bends and undercut banks. Higher up, farther away from the highway, it flows through heavy timber, features a lot of woody debris and structure and has a gorgeous canyon stretch. When you think of the perfect mountain stream, you're thinking of the upper Gibbon River. One interesting fact about the upper Gibbon: Before it was stocked with trout and adfluvial grayling, the upper river above Gibbon Falls was fishless. This extreme upper stretch, above Virginia Cascades, will now house what the park service refers to as a refuge population of west slope cutthroat trout and Arctic grayling. These cold, high-elevation drainages may be the best hope for long-term survival of fish once native to Yellowstone National Park that are in full-on recovery mode.

FLIES: Lower down, just above Virginia Cascades, I like to fish the Gibbon with small ant and beetle patterns. For years, my family has enjoyed streamside lunches on the upper Gibbon, and there are always hundreds of ants milling around. Attractor dries will most definitely work, too. Consider trying Royal Coachman, Adams and Stimulators in size 14. I can't imagine you'd ever need nymphs, but if you do, something bright and gaudy would work—try a size 16 Copper John or a size 16 bead-head Prince.

Grebe Lake

Situated atop the Gibbon River drainage, Grebe Lake is now home to restored populations of grayling and west slope cutthroat trout that were native to the Gibbon drainage but have since been extirpated. Grebe is reached via a three-and-a-half-mile trail from its trailhead on the north side of the Norris-Canyon Road. It's an easy hike, and after the new populations of cutthroats and grayling have had a chance to grow a bit, it'll be a great fishing destination.

FLIES: Start with small, weighted streamers—Woolly Buggers, Muddlers, Zonkers and the like. Grebe's features include a drop-off not too far from the bank. Anglers can wade to the edge of the drop-off and cast into the deeper water. The later in the year, the deeper the trout and grayling will be. It's totally doable to tote a float tube into Grebe Lake to make casting streamers even more effective.

Wolf Lake

Wolf Lake is easiest to access via the Grebe Lake Trail—it's about five miles using this route. Wolf Lake does have a trail of its own from the Norris-Canyon Road—a seven-mile hump through standing dead timber that burned in 1988. The bonus to taking the Wolf Lake trail? It follows the upper Gibbon to Lower Gibbon Falls before breaking off and heading to the lake through new timber coming back after the 1988 fires. It's a small lake, and the Gibbon River feeds it and drains it. The cutthroats in Wolf Lake were initially planted in 2017, with a second stocking in summer 2018. As of this writing, it's doubtful they're very big, but in a few years, this backcountry lake could be a trophy native trout factory.

FLIES: Just like Grebe Lake, I'd start with streamers. Early in the season, the fish will be cruising the edges and the drop-offs, so go with something weighted and try to cast to likely holding waters. Consider black and olive Woolly Buggers, Zonkers, Slumpbusters and Muddlers. A float tube could help, but it's a haul.

Ice Lake

Ice Lake is a small alpine lake with a seasonal connection to the upper Gibbon River. It is part of the grayling and west slope cutthroat reintroduction effort and is reachable by a short trail—less than a mile—that heads on the north side of the Norris-Canyon Road. The first west slope cutthroat were introduced into Ice Lake in August 2017, with a second planting in 2018. Grayling were stocked in the lake, too.

FLIES: Again, start with small streamers like 'Buggers and Zonkers. Evening mayfly hatches are possible—carry some size 14–16 Adams if you plan to fish later in the day. This is a short hike, and a float tube is totally doable. The fish aren't big yet, but in a year or two, Ice Lake could be a great backcountry fishery.

Goose Lake Chain of Lakes

Goose Lake is in the Firehole drainage above Firehole Falls, but it doesn't have a surface connection to the river. Today, the National Park Service uses Goose Lake to house a heritage population of pure west slope cutthroat trout that it can use for brood stock. The lakes can be reached by a biking and hiking trail that starts at the Fountain Flat parking lot. According to Koel, the lakes don't have a huge population of cutthroats, but there are some big fish in this chain of lakes.

FLIES: Once again, I'd start with streamers like black and olive Woolly Buggers and Zonkers. Because of its close proximity to the Firehole, you might keep your eyes open for a white miller caddis hatch—these clumsy bugs are common in the area, and the trout love them. It's a good dry-fly option.

9

Brown Trout

t was the first week of June, but it had been a hell of winter, so there was still quite a bit of snow atop Craig Pass as I topped the Continental Divide, heading north. Not only was there snow piled along the sides of the roads and pushed into the pullouts—to the delight of dozens of tourists—but it was also snowing pretty heavily.

It was one of those late spring squalls—fat and wet snowflakes clung to the windshield, winter's last gasp at 8,262 feet in Yellowstone.

I kept driving north, hoping against hope that the Firehole wouldn't be too high to fish with all the runoff. It's usually a dependable trout stream early in the season, and while it might take on the color of strong tea (or weak coffee, depending on your proclivities), it rarely goes through a full-on blowout. And, honestly, it fishes better in the spring, before hot weather teams up with the river's thermal inflows and warms up the river beyond the usual comfort zone for trout.

I cruised past the exit for Old Faithful as the snow turned to a light rain. I drove past the Biscuit Basin pull-off and continued north to Fountain Flat, where I knew I'd have most of the river to myself.

As I pulled up along the river, even before getting to the parking lot, I slowed my rig down to a crawl and started watching the water. Mud swallows were busy diving and darting, chasing baetis during what was clearly one of the Firehole's legendary early season Blue-winged Olive hatches. Trout rose without hesitation to duns floating along the current by the thousands. To the untrained fly-fishing eye, this was an angler's paradise.

Snow blankets Craig Pass in early June. It can snow during any month of the year in Yellowstone. *Photo by Chris Hunt.*

Except, of course, it wasn't. If you've ever experienced a Blue-winged Olive hatch like this one on the Firehole, you know that your imitation likely stands no chance when the river's browns and rainbows can choose among the literally thousands of naturals on the water. You might get a fish or two, but your odds at bringing a bunch of trout to hand when the river wears a blanket of size 20 BWOs are in the lottery range.

I pulled up into the parking lot that was mostly empty this blustery day and pulled on waders and boots. I assembled a nine-foot, 4-weight rod and walked across the short-grass meadow kept groomed by the hundreds of bison that had descended upon the valley in search of green grass. There were bison off in the distance—calving was coming to an end, and the jubilant blond babies were prancing around the adults with glee, enjoying this cool day in Yellowstone.

I got to the river after a short hike and evaluated my situation. Just as they were when I pulled up about twenty minutes earlier, swallows were busy happily chasing baetis duns as they lifted off from the river. Thousands of tiny blue-green "sailboats" floated atop the Firehole's dark surface, and the river's trout were in gluttony mode.

Rather than try to match the dry-fly hatch, I took the advice of Craig Mathews at Blue Ribbon Flies in West Yellowstone. I tied on a small BWO soft hackle, gave it a healthy dose of floatant and cast it upstream and across the river. The fly floated in the surface film, but it stood zero chance among the naturals that floated alongside it. As the fly drifted downstream and was now directly across from me, it started to pick up speed. Normally, when dry fly-fishing, this is when I throw in a mend to get a few more feet out of the drift. But with the soft-hackle bug, the fun is in the swing.

The little fly started to sprint downstream, and my line stretched out tight. Just as the fly dipped under the surface and started its swing through a subtle, but fishy, riffle, the strike came. I pulled tight to a really nice Firehole River brown trout.

As I said, this was the lesson I'd learned from Mathews years ago. Sure, it's fun to fish dry flies on the Firehole, and when hatches are sporadic, your chances are usually pretty good. But when the bugs are out, and the fish are gorging themselves on duns, sometimes it pays to cast something just a little different.

Soft-hackle imitations now occupy a fly box of their own in my sling pack. Especially when I fish the Firehole.

THE FISH

The brown trout found today in many of Yellowstone's rivers originated from two stocks: the Loch Leven brown trout from Scotland and the Von Behr strain of brown trout from Germany. Today's browns are likely a genetic mix of both strains. The common "German brown" label isn't entirely accurate for Yellowstone's European imports.

Browns of the Loch Leven strain were first planted in the upper Firehole River (which was fishless before being stocked) in 1889, and both Lewis and Shoshone Lakes got Loch Leven browns in 1890. More Loch Leven browns were planted in 1903 in Firehole River tributaries.

Also in 1890, fisheries managers in Yellowstone stocked 9,300 Von Behr–strain brown trout in Nez Perce Creek, a major tributary to the Firehole. By the time the 1921 update to *The Fishes of Yellowstone National Park* was released,

browns were known to occupy most of the length of the Firehole, including tributaries like Nez Perce Creek, the Little Firehole and Iron Creek, and also the lower Gibbon River and the entire length of the Madison River inside the park.

While this did, indeed, give anglers more opportunities—particularly above Firehole Falls—these initial plantings of nonnative trout likely signaled the beginning of the end for native west slope cutthroat trout and Arctic grayling that were native to the lower Firehole, the Gibbon and the Madison Rivers.

ABOVE: Through the fish-eye lens, a typical Firehole River rainbow trout. *Photo by Chris Hunt.*

OPPOSITE: The view from the base of Gibbon Falls on the Gibbon River. *Photo by Chris Hunt.*

THE BEST PLACES TO CATCH BROWN TROUT IN YELLOWSTONE NATIONAL PARK

The Madison River

There are resident brown trout in the Madison River, but the real treasures in the Madison are actually only part-time visitors to the river. Every fall, starting in mid- to late September and continuing through October, big brown trout—some measuring twenty-four or twenty-six inches long—migrate out of Hebgen Lake in Montana to spawn throughout the fourteen-mile stretch of the Madison inside Yellowstone. As a side note, these big browns are usually followed by rainbows from Hebgen that tag along in hopes of snacking on brown trout eggs. As you might suspect, fishing for these big fish can get a little manic—the fabled Barnes Pools just inside the west entrance to the park, accessed by a gravel road right to the river—are very popular and require some patience and tolerance of other anglers. But it's not the only place fish hold during the fall run. At nearly every pull-out along West Entrance Road as it follows the river, there is decent holding water, and the chance to catch big browns (and rainbows) is pretty good.

FLIES: Early in the season, before the fall run of the big bruisers from Hebgen, consider traditional mayfly patterns like the Green Drake in a size 14, or, during blustery, early-season days, a size 20 Blue-winged Olive for some fairly prolific baetis hatches. The Madison has a decent salmonfly hatch in early June, so don't hesitate to try big (size 8 or so) stonefly nymph imitations or even big Girdle Bugs. Later in the summer, if the river doesn't get too warm, you'll see consistent Pale Morning Dun hatches, as well

OPPOSITE, TOP: A bald eagle perches in a burned lodgepole pine tree and looks for trout in the Madison River. *Photo by Chris Hunt.*

OPPOSITE, BOTTOM: A guide and his client cast to browns and rainbows on a blustery October day on the Firehole. *Photo by Chris Hunt.*

as caddis hatches. On the upper Madison near its genesis as the Gibbon and Firehole Rivers come together, there can be good white miller caddis hatches, and the trout will go out of their way to gobble up these goofy bugs. In fall, streamers are the name of the game, and the heavier, the better. Don't be shy with these flies—some of the Kelly Galloup monster streamers, like the Sex Dungeon, the Circus Peanut and the Barely Legal, will draw aggressive strikes from the migrating browns. Also, because big rainbows often follow the browns and hover below spawning redds, don't forget your egg patterns.

The Firehole River

The Firehole might be the most consistent river for brown-trout fishing in Yellowstone, particularly early in the season and again late in the season. Early in the year, above Firehole Falls, before the weather gets too warm, browns are very active. Once summer sets in, and days are long and hot, it's probably best to leave the Firehole alone. The fish tend to retreat into cooler tributaries when warm weather couples with thermal inflows to heat the river beyond the comfort zone for most trout. Later in the year, after a good freeze or two, the river turns back on, and fishing for browns in the Firehole can be really good through October and into early November. (Fishing season in all of Yellowstone ends the first Sunday in November.)

FLIES: Early in the year, BWOs in sizes 18 and 20 are good bets, as are soft-hackles in the same pattern and sizes. PMDs start to show in early June, and dries and soft-hackles, size 16 or so, are good bets. The fabled white miller caddis also starts to pop in early summer, and these clumsy flies are delicacies for Firehole browns—Blue Ribbon Flies in West Yellowstone has some great imitations of this bug. Later in the year, consider streamers like black and olive 'Buggers and Slumpbuster in sizes 8 through 10.

The Gibbon River

The lower Gibbon River (below Gibbon Falls) actually gets a few big browns that run up out of Hebgen Lake each fall. Most of the browns that make that run don't go quite as far as the Gibbon, but the few that do are fun to chase throughout October.

One of the coolest fishing experiences an angler can have is fishing the Gibbon River directly below Gibbon Falls. From the tourist overlook above, the river looks impossible to access (and it likely is from that vantage point), but just a quarter mile or so downstream, anglers can literally step into the Gibbon from the Gibbon Falls Picnic Area. From there, it's a ten-minute walk upstream to the falls.

Higher up, above Gibbon Falls, the river runs through a long canyon stretch, and the Grand Loop Road stays pretty close to the river, offering good access. Just like the Firehole—although not to the same extent—the Gibbon is fed by a number of thermal inflows. It does get warm—sometimes too warm—in high summer, so fishing it is best left for early in the season (from the opener to early July) and again later in the season (mid-August through October).

Above the canyon stretch, the Gibbon flows through both Elk Meadows and Gibbon Meadows, and these are both great places to find large brown trout. Later in the season, toward the end of August after things have cooled off a bit, I love to float big hoppers over the undercut banks in the meadow reaches for fat and healthy brown trout.

Above the Norris Geyser basin, the river is much colder and becomes more of a meadow stream—there are some smaller browns here and likely some holdover brook trout. As efforts above Virginia Cascade continue to introduce west slope cutthroat trout and grayling, it's possible that these fish will start showing up in this stretch of the river, too, in the years to come.

FLIES: The lower Gibbon gets a good stonefly hatch in June, so big stonefly nymphs and Girdle Bugs are good bets through early July. Stonefly dries should only come out when you see naturals near the water. Like the Firehole, the Gibbon gets good BWO hatches in the spring and fall, and having these flies, size 20, in your box is a necessity (and I'd have a bunch of their soft-hackle cousins in my fly box, too). Later in the year, particularly in meadow stretches, try hoppers and other terrestrials. In Gibbon Meadows and Elk Meadows, this can be a lot of fun. Fall is streamer time—go with 'Buggers, Muddlers and Zonkers in the size 6–10 range.

The Lewis River Channel

This stretch of water between Shoshone and Lewis Lakes offers one of the coolest backcountry adventures an angler can have in Yellowstone

National Park. Every fall, usually starting in early October and continuing until the park closes to fishing on the first Sunday in November, big browns from both lakes congregate in this short but stunning stretch of river to spawn. Often, they are joined by lake trout, which spawn close to the inlet and outlet of the channel.

There are two ways to get to the channel: one takes you to the channel as it leaves Shoshone Lake, and one takes you to where the channel enters Lewis Lake. Both destinations will sport migrating brown trout. It's about a four-and-a half-mile trudge to the outlet on Shoshone Lake from the Dogshead Trailhead along the Grand Loop Road south of Grant Village. The Lewis River Trail starts at the same trailhead and goes three miles to the channel. It's totally doable, if you leave early in the day, to hike to the outlet, fish downstream to where the channel empties into Lewis Lake and then hike out on the Lewis River Trail and be back by dark. There is a backcountry campsite at the Shoshone Lake outlet.

FLIES: Streamers, streamers, streamers. And when you're done with streamers, go with egg patterns. The Lewis River Channel is all but barren in the spring and summer. It really only comes to life when the fall-spawning brown trout enter the river in October and when lake trout from both Lewis and Shoshone Lakes spawn near the inlet and outlet. There's no need for delicacy or light fly rods here. In fact, this may be the only place in the park where I'd consider using a 7-weight rod, as you'll be casting big streamers, like size 4 'Buggers and Zonkers. And, you'll be casting to large fish—both the browns and the lake trout regularly eclipse twenty inches.

OPPOSITE, TOP: The Lewis River Channel connects Shoshone Lake with Lewis Lake, and is a great place to go for brown trout and lake trout in the fall. *Photo by Chris Hunt.*

OPPOSITE, BOTTOM: Rachel Andona casts in the shallows of Shoshone Lake for lake trout and brown trout in October. *Photo by Chris Hunt.*

OTHER NOTABLE BROWN TROUT DESTINATIONS IN YELLOWSTONE NATIONAL PARK

The **LEWIS RIVER** below Lewis Falls is a great destination for wild browns, but it's really only accessible directly below the falls and then again as it flows out of the Lewis River Canyon and flows into the Snake River. Browns in the canyon stretch can get to about seventeen inches, but most will be in the twelve-inch range.

The lower **GARDNER RIVER** in the park's northwest corner is home to a solid population of wild browns, along with rainbows, cuttbows and whitefish. The lower five miles of the Gardner are easily accessed via a number of pull-outs and short trailheads between Mammoth and Northeast Entrance to the park.

NEZ PERCE CREEK is a major tributary to the Firehole—it flows into the bigger river below Fountain Flat. While you can fish the creek from where it crosses under the Grand Loop Road both upstream and downstream, the best fishing can be accessed via the Mary Mountain Trail just south of where the creek flows under the highway. It's about a mile walk to the creek, but the trail follows the creek for many miles more into the backcountry, and you'll likely find that, in its upper reaches above a series of thermal inflows, Nez Perce Creek is much cooler than the Firehole—this is one of the destinations for Firehole brown trout seeking to escape hot summer temperatures.

THE LITTLE FIREHOLE RIVER flows into the Firehole above Biscuit Basin and can be accessed via the Continental Divide Trail. There are browns in the lower river, below the seventy-foot Mystic Falls, and in the upper river, where the browns are joined by some wild brook trout. Lower river browns will be bigger, up to fifteen inches or so. Upper river browns will be more numerous and, thanks to cooler water, can be pursued all summer long.

OPPOSITE: Cameron Hunt shows off a nice Nez Perce Creek brown trout. *Photo by Chris Hunt.*

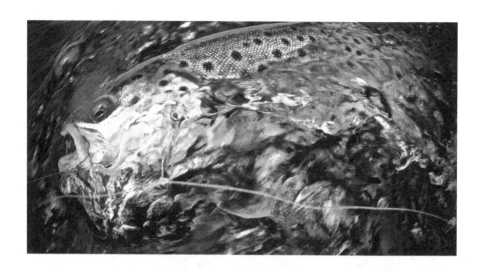

TOP: A typical Firehole River brown trout caught on opening weekend in Yellowstone National Park. *Photo by Chris Hunt.*

BOTTOM: A brown trout from below Gibbon Falls. *Photo by Chris Hunt.*

Shoshone Lake just as it flows
into the Lewis River Channel.
Photo by Chris Hunt.

IRON SPRING CREEK starts as two forks that start in the backcountry southwest of Old Faithful. The stream, where the two forks come together above Black Sand Basin, can be accessed from the Grand Loop Road. While the Little Firehole stays cooler in the summer, Iron Spring Creek has lots of thermal inflows, so it's best fished for its wild browns in the spring and fall.

SENTINEL CREEK is a tributary to the Firehole—it hits the river near Fountain Flat Drive. Sentinel Creek's lower reaches fish much like the Firehole, meaning it will be better in the spring and fall. However, its upper reaches, above all the thermal inflows, fish well all summer, and Firehole River browns use Sentinel Creek as a thermal refuge in the summer.

SHOSHONE CREEK enters Shoshone Lake on its western edge. It's a haul to get into Shoshone Creek, but it does have a few nice browns, particularly in the fall. The best way to access it is via the Dogshead Trailhead—follow Shoshone Lake Trail four miles to where the Lewis River channel starts. Ford the channel and then go another eight miles (yes, it's a haul, and not a day hike). You can also get to it via the Lone Star Trailhead, but you'll have to top the Continental Divide. Also, not a day hike.

ROBINSON CREEK flows off the Pitchstone Plateau into Idaho, and there are brown trout here, as well as cuttbows, rainbows, brook trout and mountain whitefish. It's best accessed via a bushwhack from Idaho's Horseshoe Lake. The hike requires a dive into a steep canyon where Robinson Creek flows out of Yellowstone National Park into Idaho, and, of course, a steep climb out. This is not for the faint of heart.

10
Brook Trout

You don't waste beautiful October days in Yellowstone, particularly when it's already snowed a couple of times and reminded you that winter is really, really close.

As I trudged down the DeLacy Creek trail toting a glass 2-weight rod and a box of dry flies, I knew I was stealing weather on this brilliantly bright and warm day. Two days earlier, snow had pounded West Yellowstone. The day before, the sun came out, and I and a buddy of mine popped in on a beer festival and generally drank a beautiful afternoon away. I was wracked with guilt—sunny and in the sixties in West Yellowstone? In mid-October?

I should have been fishing.

So this day, after waking up with a righteous craft-beer hangover, it would have served me right to have the snow move in again and effectively put an end to the season's fishing in the world's first national park. But it just wasn't the case. The sun came out, just like it had the day before. The mercury started climbing. By the time I got a big breakfast inside of me and probably a gallon of coffee for good measure, it was downright pleasant.

So I grabbed my creek gear, drove to the DeLacy Creek trailhead south of Old Faithful and started walking downstream. My target? Handsome brook trout wearing the orange, blue and green spawning tuxedos they don each fall.

Now, for perspective, the brookies in DeLacy Creek are usually quite small when anglers chase them during the summer months. The creek is small, too, as it winds its way south to Shoshone Lake. But in fall, brookies

An October brook trout from lower DeLacy Creek. *Photo by Chris Hunt.*

that I honestly believe use Shoshone Lake for summer thermal relief move into DeLacy Creek and make their way upstream in pods of dozens. They're not huge, but it's possible to get into foot-long brook trout, and that's a trophy for a fish that tends to overpopulate small mountain streams and then become stunted.

And, after just a short hike into the backcountry—maybe halfway to the trail's end at Shoshone Lake—I could hear the brook trout frolicking in the nearby creek. I carefully stepped off the trail into a meadow stretch of the stream and slowly poked my head over the October-brown grass along the stream. There, finning in the current, was a pod of about thirty char native to the cold, clear streams of Appalachia, holding like miniature salmon. Every now and then, a fish would break from the pod and swim up a short riffle—it's what passes as rapids on this tiny, little-known creek.

I flipped a size 14 Adams over the edge of the grass, where it landed just upstream of the riffle. I couldn't see the fly, but I could tell it raised a commotion among the staging fish—the sound of splashes was followed by my line going tight, and seconds later, I was releasing what I believe to be the most beautiful fish ever put on this planet.

Brookies start to stage for the fall spawn in September, and they'll get into the spawning attire pretty quickly. I've caught lots of September brook trout, and I used to think nothing was more gorgeous. I was wrong. October brook trout are simply stunning.

I spent the afternoon spotting and stalking pods of interloping brookies, bringing several fish to hand that I know don't spend their summers in this skinny water. A couple exceeded twelve inches in length, and the last fish of the day was a stunning fourteen-inch brook trout that simply made me want to "drop the mic" and hike home.

It wouldn't get any better than that.

Author's note: I write about DeLacy with mixed feelings. While there are no immediate plans to remove the stream's nonnative brook trout, DeLacy is listed in the park's Native Fish Conservation Plan for potential Yellowstone cutthroat introduction. While I more than understand the need to bring native fish back to the park and create populations where none existed before to ensure their long-term survival, part of me will miss these stunning, exotic gems, if and when the park service decides to treat DeLacy Creek and remove the brookies.

THE FISH

Brook trout are actually a char, like lake trout, Dolly Varden, bull trout and Arctic char, and they're native to Appalachia, the Driftless streams of the upper Midwest, the lakes and rivers of Ontario, New Brunswick, Nova Scotia and Labrador. There are even brook trout that use saltwater estuaries in the Northeast from Cape Cod to Maine and north into Canada.

They are not native to the West but have been propagated throughout the Rockies and the Sierra, where they are certainly more abundant than they are in their native Appalachian Mountains stretching from north Georgia to Maine and on up into Canada. In Yellowstone, brookies were among the first nonnative trout to be stocked, and they quickly overtook many small streams and backcountry lakes from native cutthroat trout.

According to Kendall's 1914 report, brookies were first introduced in 1889 in the Gardner River and in the West Fork of the Gardner River in

1890. The National Park Service also contends that brook trout were the first nonnative trout introduced to the park when they were placed into the Firehole River above Firehole Falls in 1889.

Given that brookies require the cleanest and coldest waters to survive and thrive, any remnant populations of this initial stocking are now almost certainly living higher up in the cold-water tributaries of the Firehole. They do still thrive in the upper and middle reaches of the Gardner and its tributaries.

Brookies don't intermingle with any native fish come spawning season. They are fall spawners, and cutthroat trout spawn in the spring. However, because they are fall spawners and their young emerge over the course of the winter, they have an advantage over cutthroat fry that don't emerge until late spring or early summer in some instances. Brook trout simply outcompete native cutthroats in nearly every river or stream where both can be found (or, more accurately, where brookies are and cutthroats are no longer).

Brookies will literally eat themselves out of habitat. In austere mountain streams, rather than spawning less or producing fewer eggs as a result of limited resources, brookies simply stunt and become big populations of very small fish. A spawning-age brookie in a stunted population might be three or four years old and measure less than six inches long.

This is largely true in Yellowstone, in most instances. However, it is possible, in a place or two, to catch trophy-sized brook trout. But you'll have to work for it.

THE BEST PLACES TO CATCH BROOK TROUT IN YELLOWSTONE NATIONAL PARK

The Gardner River

The upper reaches of the Gardner River, above Indian Creek Campground on the Grand Loop Road south of Mammoth, is a great place to find small- to mid-sized brook trout all summer long and into the fall. Here, the Gardner, Panther Creek and Indian Creek all come together within a few hundred yards of one another. You can reach the upper Gardner by parking above

A brook trout from the upper Gardner River. *Photo by Chris Hunt.*

or below the bridge as the river flows under the highway, or you can park in the campground if it's not too busy. Fishing for prolific and aggressive brook trout is good both upstream and downstream of the bridge.

Lower, as the Gardner flows through Sheepeater Canyon, fishing for bigger brook trout in the eight-to-ten-inch range can be good in the pocket water. There's a chance you'll pick up the odd rainbow, too.

FLIES: As with most brook trout waters in the park, the flies aren't terribly important. Anything that looks like food will likely get a look from hungry brook trout, so rather than try to please the fish, I try to please my aging eyes and use flies I can see, like high-floating stimulators and small terrestrials, regardless of the time of year. Brookies will hit small streamers and soft-hackles on the swing, too, so if that's your thing, go with small 'Buggers in a size 10 or so, or swing soft-hackles, like a size 12 Hornberg or San Juan King through the faster water on the Gardner. It can be fun.

Grizzly Lake and Straight Creek

The Grizzly Lake Trail starts on the Grand Loop Road south of the moose exhibit on the west side of the highway. You'll essentially be in the Obsidian Creek headwaters and you'll hike northwest over a pretty decent rise. You'll then drop down into the neighboring valley—the trail will deposit you at the mouth of Straight Creek as it flows out of Grizzly Lake. The brookies in the creek are pretty tiny—six to eight inches long, generally. But, the closer you get to the outlet of Grizzly Lake, the bigger the fish get. In late summer and fall, bigger brookies from Grizzly Lake move down into Straight Creek to spawn. These fish can be a foot long or longer.

FLIES: For the creek, go with a fly you can see, like a high-riding Wulff or Coachman. Cast up and across and let the fly drift as naturally as possible. If you don't get a strike on the drift, let the fly swing out below you and skate. If you still don't get a strike, move to a different spot. If you like to swing small streamers or soft-hackles, go for it. For the lake, you should consider small, weighted streamers stripped slowly through the dark water along the edges. The lake will fish best in early summer and again in the fall.

Joffe Lake

Joffe Lake is actually little more than a pond, but it's accessible by car via Wonderland Road south of Mammoth. You'll have to drive through the Yellowstone Youth Conservation Corps complex and some residential housing for park employees, but the road generally ends at Joffe Lake. The brookies in Joffe get a little bigger than they do in the neighboring streams, and it's possible to catch fish up to twelve or thirteen inches. Joffe will fish best just after opening day and again later in the season.

FLIES: Small streamers would be my first bet—olive or brown 'Buggers or even something that might resemble a damselfly nymph, like a Stayner Ducktail, should work well.

Lava Creek

Lava Creek's brook-trout section is above Undine Falls and is best accessed from a picnic area just off the Grand Loop Road southeast of Mammoth. Lava Creek is a beautiful little mountain stream that winds through the timber and houses small to medium-sized brook trout in the six-to-ten-inch range. It only takes a bend or two in the creek to get away from whatever crowds are in the picnic area, and it's possible to spend all day fishing this nice-sized stream for enthusiastic brookies. It's a great place to take kids, too—the brookies are willing.

FLIES: The broken record continues. Attractor dries. If you must swing streamers, make them small. Personally, I'd tie on a size 14 Adams and I wouldn't change flies until I lost it, or until it became unrecognizable after being chewed on all day long.

Blacktail Deer Creek

I'm not sure how this stream got its name—I've never seen a black-tail deer anywhere near Yellowstone. According to the document *Historical Origins of Waterways Names in Yellowstone*, historian Hiram Chittenden claimed the creek was named prior to 1870 because the area was, indeed, home to black-tail deer. (I've yet to find a biological reference that confirms this. It's possible the critters were really mule deer, as black-tail deer aren't found here.)

Nevertheless, the creek is home to a robust population of brook trout that top out at about ten inches. The stream crosses under the Grand Loop Road east of Mammoth and flows off the Blacktail Plateau. Of note, the park service prevents access to the Black Tail area south of the Grand Loop Road due to frequent grizzly bear activity until June 30. The downstream side of the road is open, but use caution and carry bear spray.

FLIES: Blacktail runs quick, especially early in the year, so I like to fish it downstream on the swing with small nymphs or streamers. Later in the year, as water levels come down, it's dry-fly time, and small terrestrials will keep you—and the creek's little brookies—entertained for as long as you wish.

Tower Creek

You may be intimidated by the typical summer melee surrounding the pull-off at Tower Fall as you travel between Canyon and Roosevelt. The little convenience store is always packed. Parking takes a special brand of patience, and you'll need to be tolerant of the visitors milling around like mad in hopes of getting that perfect photo of Tower Fall as it dives 132 feet over a cliff into the Grand Canyon of the Yellowstone. But once you find a place to park and assemble a sweet little 3-weight rig, walk upstream on the Tower Creek Trail and you'll be away from it all.

Tower Creek might be my favorite brook-trout stream in Yellowstone, and once you leave the throngs behind, you'll be gloriously alone. Tower Creek is exactly what you think a trout stream should look like, with deep runs, tight corners, undercut banks and lots and lots of fishy structure. That it's full of only small brook trout might be disappointing, but fishing up into the canyon above the falls is an experience you won't ever forget. But, just in case, bring your bear spray.

Of note: The lower reaches of Tower Creek below the falls requires a steep hike down, but, after the July 15 opener, you might get into some cutthroats running up out of the Yellowstone River that can reach sixteen to eighteen inches in length. It's a grueling hike out, though.

FLIES: Attractor dries once again make the most sense, and not so much because the fish can see them, but because you can see them. Tower Creek runs through a canyon, and there are some fast-water stretches that can make seeing your fly tough if it doesn't float high and dry. You can try streamers and soft-hackles here, but, honestly, you'll have more fun catching fat and happy brookies on dry flies.

Fawn Lake

The only reason I mention Fawn Lake here is that it is rumored to hold truly big brook trout in the twenty-plus-inch range—Koel has confirmed this, but he's unsure of the size of the fish of late. I do know that Fawn Lake is tough to fish because it's surrounded by either marsh or heavy timber, and the small lake endures prolific weed growth over the course of a summer. It can be accessed by the Glen Creek Trail off the Grand Loop Road southwest of

Mammoth. It's a two-mile hike on the Glen Creek Trail to the Fawn Lake Trail, and then three miles to the lake itself—probably a bit too far, even for die-hard anglers, to get to with a float tube.

FLIES: I'd start with the obvious streamers, and I'd fish the creek as early in the year as possible so I wouldn't have to deal with all the weeds as summer progresses. Consider 'Buggers in black and olive, weighted Zonkers, Muddlers and Slumpbusters. Keep an eye out for evening mayfly hatches—carry some size 14 Adams patterns in, just in case.

OTHER NOTABLE BROOK TROUT DESTINATIONS IN YELLOWSTONE NATIONAL PARK

GLEN CREEK is accessed from the Glen Creek Trailhead southwest of Mammoth, just off the Grand Loop Road. It has small but enthusiastic brook trout. It runs under the Grand Loop Road and then dives over Rustic Falls through Golden Gate Canyon. This lower stretch is tough to reach, unless you have some mountain goat genes in the family.

OBSIDIAN CREEK is the really pretty meadow creek you'll see on the west side of the Grand Loop Road as you drive between Norris and Mammoth below Beaver Lake. The brookies are tiny. But there are lots of them.

WINTER CREEK joins Straight Creek about a mile downstream from Grizzly Lake. It's home to a lot of eight-inch brook trout.

INDIAN CREEK flows into the upper Gardner River right at the Indian Creek Campground southwest of Mammoth. Lots of little brookies. Great place to take kids.

PANTHER CREEK comes into the upper Gardner from the west, just above Indian Creek Campground. It's home to a good population of small brook trout.

The **GIBBON RIVER** below Virginia Cascade has historically been a dependable place to catch brook trout. The upper river has been treated to remove all nonnative brookies and rainbows, and it has been restocked with native west slope cutthroat trout and grayling. Below the Norris Geyser Basin, the Gibbon is mostly brown-trout water. The stretch between Virginia Cascade and the geyser basin may be the last dependable place on the Gibbon to catch brook trout.

The upper reaches of **SODA BUTTE CREEK** now have brook trout, much to the disappointment of Yellowstone's fisheries team. The silver lining? Brookies are delicious, and this is a great place for anglers to visit and keep all the brook trout they catch (while releasing all native cutthroat trout, please).

DELACY CREEK flows into Shoshone Lake from the north and is accessible via the DeLacy Creek Trail south of Old Faithful on the Grand Loop Road. It's home to really small brookies, at least until fall, when larger brook trout move up in the system to spawn.

MOOSE CREEK flows into Shoshone Lake from the south and can be accessed by the Shoshone Lake Trail at the Dogshead Trailhead of the Grand Loop Road south of Grant Village. It's home to small brookies, but, in the fall, it gets a run of browns. That said, to get to it in the fall, you'd have to ford the Lewis River Channel. I'm not sure it's worth another two miles of hiking to catch fish smaller than the fish in the channel.

The **LEWIS RIVER** below Lewis Lake does have brook trout, but it's also home to larger browns. I wouldn't fish here with the idea of catching brookies, but rather as a bonus while looking for browns that can be fifteen inches and bigger.

FISH LAKE sits just outside the south boundary of Yellowstone National Park; you'll need a Wyoming license to fish it. The only reason I mention it is because there are some really big brookies here—some to eighteen or even twenty inches. You can get to it from Fish Lake Road off of Reclamation Road. It's a short hike, totally doable with a float tube. It fishes best after ice-out, and again in the fall. In the summer, the fish are deep.

The **FALL RIVER** does have a few brookies in it, particularly around Cave Falls, where they tend to occupy the slower margins of the river.

ROBINSON CREEK is home to small brook trout that live among browns, rainbows, cutthroats, cuttbows and mountain whitefish. It's accessed via steep bushwhack from Horseshoe Lake on the far southwest border of the park with Idaho. It's a beast of a hike out.

OPPOSITE, TOP: A mule deer buck in velvet is surprised in the willows on the upper Gardner River. *Photo by Chris Hunt.*

OPPOSITE, BOTTOM: Volunteers shock upper Soda Butte Creek for invasive brook trout. *Photo by Chris Hunt.*

NEZ PERCE CREEK, a major tributary to the Firehole, is home to brookies in its upper reaches. To get to the brook trout water, use the Mary Mountain Trail, which starts north of where the creek crosses under the Grand Loop Road north of Old Faithful. It eventually joins the creek, but you'll have to walk a couple miles to get above the thermal inflows. That's when brookies will start to show up.

SENTINEL CREEK is home to brookies in its upper stretches. It flows into the Firehole in a meadow across from Fountain Flat parking area. The farther you hike up the creek, the more likely you'll be to find brook trout.

The **LITTLE FIREHOLE RIVER** has some brook trout above Mystic Falls. It's best accessed via the Biscuit Basin Trailhead. It's about a third of mile to the falls, which is where I'd start fishing if I were looking for brookies.

The **FIREHOLE RIVER** above Kepler Cascades south of Old Faithful holds brook trout that can climb to about ten inches long. The best way to access this stretch of the Firehole is via the Lone Star Geyser Trail, which is open to bicycles. It's a great place to ride your mountain bike and cover lots of water.

OPPOSITE, TOP: Cave Falls stretches across the Fall River in the southwest corner of Yellowstone National Park. *Photo by Rachel Andona.*

OPPOSITE, BOTTOM: Nez Perce Creek is a tributary to the Firehole River and fishes great in its upper reaches for browns, rainbows and brook trout all summer long. *Photo by Chris Hunt.*

11
Lake Trout

For a closet introvert who can fake the opposite on command, time alone is like being plugged into a battery charger.

If only I had a USB port at the back of my neck. Then I wouldn't need to disappear for hours at a time to replenish what the real world drains. (On second thought, when that port is invented, please pass me by—I'm not interested.)

While "alone time" is necessary for a guy like me, there are times when a friendly voice is appreciated. As I hiked on blistered feet out of the Yellowstone backcountry, racing the sunset and losing miserably, I would have loved a reassuring voice, if for nothing else than to have a little conversation to discourage the park's grizzlies from getting the wrong idea.

I stayed and fished at my destination—the outlet of Shoshone Lake where it dumps into the Lewis River Channel—far too long. I took an inexplicable wrong turn down a spur trail that likely cost me two miles. And, despite my belief to the contrary, I didn't pack a headlamp. As the sun set over the skeletal lodgepole trunks left over from the fires of 1988, I knew I was going to have to hump it to make the trailhead before the light gave out entirely. In the distance, the bugle of a rutting bull elk was countered by the mournful howl of a wolf. Soon, other big canines joined in, and the elk, wisely, ceased his call. Off in the trees in the half-light of deep dusk, something big stepped on crunchy ground and moved away from the sound of my footsteps on the trail.

As I walked the last mile and a half while holding the LCD screen of my digital camera out in front of me for an inkling of light, I knew that being alone—while therapeutic and ultimately healthful—was pretty risky. Thankfully, I'd managed to navigate the "moderate" portion of the hike in the failing light of day. The home stretch is pretty flat and unremarkable, although I still stumbled a few times before I made it to the truck.

After a sans socks summer of sandals, my feet rebelled at the notion of my hiking boots. Six miles into a twelve-mile round-tripper, I knew I might be in trouble. By the time the hike mercifully ended, I was sporting ripe blisters on both pinky toes, and my feet were...hot.

After I dumped my pack and my rod case in the back, I climbed thankfully into the driver's seat of my trusty FJ Cruiser. I'd stashed a turkey sandwich, a liter of water and a couple of apples in a brown paper bag under the passenger seat, and all were gone within minutes.

The chill that comes with sunset in Yellowstone started to set in over the last half of the hike out, but I was prepared for it with layers and, of course, a cardiovascular counterweight to autumn's chill—six miles up and over a ridge or two at about seven thousand feet will keep anyone's blood pumping.

ABOVE: A lake trout takes a gaudy streamer in the Lewis River Channel just below the Shoshone Lake outlet. *Photo by Chris Hunt.*

OPPOSITE: A lake trout from the outlet of Shoshone Lake as it flows into the Lewis River Channel. *Photo by Chris Hunt.*

As I sat in the car, relieved and a little regretful that I couldn't fish a bit longer in this amazing place, I began to feel the night settle in around me. It was a cavalier move—hiking all that way and staying too long, alone.

Not my best work.

But a tight fly line and the rare chance to connect with fish that only visit the shallows at certain times of the year inspired this adventure, and this was the day I'd set aside for it. Lake trout on the fly. Beefy, fish-eating char with appetites so voracious they can wipe out indigenous fish and then turn on each other for sustenance.

No regrets. None.

And the battery is replenished. No USB required.

Editor's note: The above essay first appeared on the author's former personal blog, Eat More Brook Trout.

THE FISH

Lake trout are the great villain in the effort to restore and reintroduce native cutthroat trout to their natal waters within Yellowstone National Park. These voracious natives of the Great Lakes and the deep potholes of the Precambrian Shield far to the north were first brought to Yellowstone in 1890 and introduced into Shoshone and Lewis Lakes, and later in Heart Lake. Both Shoshone and Heart Lakes are backcountry lakes with no road access. Lewis Lake can be reached along the Grand Loop Road.

And while the story of lake trout in Yellowstone is still being told—with the climax hopefully coming in the late first decade of this century, when the big char that had initially been discovered in Yellowstone Lake in 1994 officially crashed the native cutthroat trout population—I am considering a new perspective.

OPPOSITE: Sunset on the Shoshone Lake Trail, Yellowstone National Park. *Photo by Chris Hunt.*

TOP: The author fishes the emerald shallows of Shoshone Lake for migrating lake trout. *Photo by Rachel Andona.*

BOTTOM: A nice lake trout comes to hand in Shoshone Lake. Lakers come into the shallows in the spring and fall. *Photo by Chris Hunt.*

Yes, the illegal/accidental introduction of lakers into Yellowstone Lake—the last true big-water refuge for pure Yellowstone cutthroat trout—was and remains an ecological tragedy. That, with an all-hands-on-deck effort, we've been able to largely bring the cutthroats back by netting, monitoring, tracking and killing lake trout is nothing short of a miracle.

But lake trout gave Yellowstone a foil, a reason to rally behind native fish, and not just the native fish in Yellowstone Lake. The lake trout invasion gave fisheries experts like Todd Koel a reason to take a deeper dive into the park's native trout tapestry and to really work to propagate not only the fisheries restoration efforts that are underway in Yellowstone today but also the political environment under which such an ambitious plan could even be executed.

Think about it. Sure, it's possible that, had lake trout never found their way into Yellowstone Lake, the National Park Service would have dutifully begun working on larger native trout and Arctic grayling recovery projects in the park. But would this effort have been so inspired if not for the invasive predator that, at one time, had managed to eliminate 99 percent of the spawning cutthroat trout from Yellowstone Lake? Would this ambitious and incredibly progressive plan to bring natives back to watersheds where they had been extirpated—sometimes for as long as a century—been greeted so enthusiastically by park service brass, the Department of the Interior, Congress and the American public if lake trout hadn't proven what happens when the worst-case scenario comes true?

I think the answer is no. I think the lake trout invasion in Yellowstone woke up all of us angler-conservationists. I think it inspired biologists to become advocates for native trout in the world's first national park, to right the wrongs done early in the park's management process. I think there was a great admission on the part of agency bureaucrats, politicians and, yes, anglers, that we haven't always known what's best for our rivers and and streams and the special places like Yellowstone. And now that we know better, it's time we *do* better.

So, yes, the lake trout is Yellowstone's villain. But without a villain there can be no hero. Who's the hero? This story is still being told.

THE BEST PLACES TO CATCH LAKE TROUT IN YELLOWSTONE NATIONAL PARK

Yellowstone Lake

Let's start with the obvious. This is ground zero for perhaps the biggest ecological disaster to ever involve native trout in the United States. (We could argue that the Great Lakes might have a case for something similar, however, given the ecological torture they have endured for the better part of two hundred years.) How lake trout ended up in Yellowstone Lake is anybody's guess, but everybody now knows they don't belong there. And while millions of lake trout have been removed from the signature body of water in our first national park over the last fifteen years or so (in 2017, more than 360,000 lake trout were netted and removed), there are still lots of big *Salvelinus namaycush* lying in wait in Yellowstone Lake's depths.

On average, each adult fish will eat forty Yellowstone cutthroat trout in a year. It doesn't help, of course, that lake trout are hard to get to with even conventional fishing tackle. They live in the deepest, coldest water most of the year, only coming into the shallows in the spring right after ice-out, and again in the fall to spawn. This gives us fly-fishers a pretty tight window to get after these big predators.

But it's possible. If you have a boat, it's really doable. In the fall, lake trout spawn in the shallows around the West Thumb in places like the shallows near Carrington Island and near the mouth of Solution Creek. The

Volunteers pick lake trout from gillnets stretched in Yellowstone Lake using telemetry data that tells biologists where the invasive trout are likely to be at any given time of the year. *Photo by Chris Hunt.*

National Park Service is documenting new spawning sites using "Judas" fish that have been implanted with telemetry receivers. These fish send signals back to the telemetry equipment, which is monitored by the park service to determine where fish are, when they're using certain habitat and, most important, where they go in the fall to spawn. One note: it is illegal to release a live lake trout in Yellowstone Lake. In other words, if you catch one, fire up the smoker.

FLIES: With the understanding that you have to get deep to get to lake trout, even during the fall spawn, I'd recommend going with sink-tip, or even full-sink lines when casting from shore, and full-sink lines when casting from boats. And you'll want to throw big streamers that can move water and get the attention of spawning fish. Consider Kelly Galloup's ever-growing library of big, gnarly streamers—they're perfect for lake trout.

But don't forget the simple favorites, fished deep. I've caught lake trout in the shallows on Halloween Leeches, orange and yellow Woolly Buggers and other streamers that are a bit gaudy and might represent a threat to spawning fish.

Shoshone Lake

The best way to get to Shoshone Lake is via the Dogshead Trailhead south of Old Faithful on the South Entrance Road. It's a four-and-a-half-mile hike to the lake and the mouth of the Lewis River Channel. Starting toward the end of September and on into October, you can actually see lake trout staging and getting ready to spawn in the crystal-clear lake as it prepares to empty into the channel. The last time I was at the outlet, there were several pairs of lake trout actually in the channel itself, in calm but moving water no more than two feet deep just starting to dig spawning redds. Starting around the middle of October, brown trout will be moving down out of Shoshone Lake to spawn, too, giving anglers a really great opportunity to catch big trout in a stunning backcountry setting.

You can also get to Shoshone Lake via the three-and-a-half-mile DeLacy Creek Trail, and I have caught lakers in the shallows there. But the bottom of the lake is fine sand at the mouth of DeLacy Creek—not ideal for spawning fish. My suspicion is that lake trout will stage and spawn in the shallower stream inlets all around Shoshone Lake so long as there is good spawning gravel mixed with larger cobble. Anglers willing to put in the work can find them in these places and sight-cast to them in the fall. Lakers will also come into the shallows in the spring, just after ice-out, cruising the warmer water in search of prey.

FLIES: Again, big streamers that push water and make a racket will give you the best shot at staging and spawning lake trout. While lakers will eat before and during the fall spawn, the real goal is to trigger their protective and competitive instincts and get them to strike out of anger and aggression.

Lewis Lake

The Lewis Lake Trail starts at the same Dogshead Trailhead where the Shoshone Lake Trail starts off the Grand Loop Road south of Old Faithful.

It's a quick and easy three-mile hike to where the Lewis River Channel empties into Lewis Lake. Lake trout are known to stage and spawn in the lower end of the channel itself, as well as in the shallows on the fringes of the outlet, but still in the lake.

Lewis Lake features a lot of "benches," or shallow gravel beds that drop off to deeper water all around the lake. By accessing the lake at the Lewis Lake Campground at the lower end of the lake, anglers can fish the entire eastern shoreline of the lake, and they can ford the Lewis River at the outlet (also a potential lake trout staging and spawning area) and fish up the west shore, too.

Like in Shoshone Lake and in Yellowstone Lake, the lake trout will come into the shallows just after ice-out and cruise the sun-warmed waters for bait. Both spring and fall offer the best chances at big lakers in Lewis Lake.

FLIES: I'd spend some quality time at Blue Ribbon Flies in West Yellowstone, plucking the biggest, ugliest streamers from the fly trays. Just as in the lakes mentioned above, big flies that move water will get their attention. Fish them as deep as you can and vary your retrieve until you find the sweet spot.

Heart Lake

Heart Lake has both native cutthroat trout and lake trout, and the National Park Service requires anglers catching lake trout in Heart Lake to kill their catch. For novice anglers, telling the two fish apart might not be as easy as you think. The simple way to tell a char from a cutthroat is that char (lake trout) have light spots and markings on dark bodies. Trout have dark spots and markings on light bodies. Cutthroats, of course, will sport the bright red slash under their jaws that gives them their name. As for fishing for lake trout, the park usually keeps the Heart Lake Trail closed until June 30, because it's a really active grizzly bear zone, so spring fishing is probably out.

Consider fishing it in the fall. (Honestly, if you tried to get to Heart Lake in June, you'd probably be walking through some serious snow drifts.) Heart Lake features a couple of notable inlet streams on its north shore, and the Heart River runs out of the lake at its southeast corner. This is where lakers will stage and spawn in the fall. The best way to get to Heart Lake is via the Heart Lake Trail, which starts on the east side of the South Entrance Road south of Grant Village. It's a seven-and-a-half-mile hike to Heart Lake, and it's a doozy, as you must hike over Factory Hill and then drop down to the lake. Consider this before you make the commitment.

FLIES: Big, gaudy flies that push water will be your best bet on Heart Lake. When lake trout occupy the same water as cutthroat trout, I like to add a little orange or red to the flies I fish.

12

The "Other" Fish

A s noted above, there are other wild fish in Yellowstone National Park, and they're worth your time if you're simply interested in casting to willing trout or whitefish in Yellowstone's awe-inspiring settings.

For instance, the rainbow-cutthroat hybrid, or the "cuttbow," is found in many places in Yellowstone, but particularly in the park's northwest corner in streams like **BACON RIND CREEK**, the upper reaches of the **GALLATIN RIVER** and the gorgeous little trout stream that is **FAN CREEK**. Cuttbows are also common in the park's southwest corner in the upper reaches of the **BECHLER RIVER**, **ROBINSON CREEK**, **BOUNDARY CREEK**, **MOUNTAIN ASH CREEK** and the higher reaches of the **FALL RIVER**.

If you're interested in mountain whitefish, your best bet is going to be the park's bigger, colder waters, like the **YELLOWSTONE RIVER**, the **LAMAR RIVER**, the **LEWIS RIVER** and the **SNAKE RIVER**. These natives are most closely related to Arctic grayling, and they've been known to save many a trout trip when the more "desirable" rainbows, browns and cutthroats failed to show up. It's important to note that whitefish are not trash fish—they are a true Yellowstone sport fish, and their presence generally means that the water you're fishing is cold and clean and just right for the trout you might be after.

I like to fish for whitefish in the winter months—they're more active than trout in colder water. Yellowstone, of course, closes to fishing in early November and doesn't reopen until the last Saturday in May, so winter fly-

A mountain whitefish from the lower Lewis River. *Photo by Chris Hunt.*

fishing isn't an option. But if you find yourself in a gateway community in winter and absolutely *must* fly-fish, you have some great whitefish options.

The **MADISON RIVER** below Hebgen Dam holds big whitefish, as does the **YELLOWSTONE RIVER** below Gardiner. The **SNAKE RIVER** through Grand Teton National Park (which is subject to Wyoming fishing regulations) has a very healthy whitefish population as it runs all the way through Wilson, Wyoming, and south of Jackson to its confluence with the Hoback River. The **SHOSHONE RIVER** east of the park has whitefish, too.

13

A Note on America's Public Lands

J ust like every other national park, national forest, national grassland or swath of Bureau of Land Management acreage in the United States or within its commonwealth, Yellowstone belongs to you. It's administered on your behalf by the National Park Service, which is part of the U.S. Department of the Interior. It's not "government land." It's your land. You own it. Your taxes fund its upkeep, its maintenance and a good portion of the work the park service is doing to restore and protect its native fish.

Only in America is this the case. Public ownership of a shared estate was a new idea in the late 1800s and early 1900s, when thoughtful people like Theodore Roosevelt and Gifford Pinchot essentially put forth the notion that every American enjoys a single birthright: a common interest in the country's vast, rich estate of undeveloped land. These were—and still are—the places where Americans could visit and enjoy, where they could fish, hunt, hike, camp and climb. These are the places where no free man need seek permission to pursue the "king's deer," where anyone, anytime could simply wander the wilds, lose track of time and perhaps find their souls.

For generations, this birthright was largely assumed, perhaps even taken for granted. I know, as a kid, when I'd camp and fish with my grandfathers in the wilds of Colorado's Rocky Mountains, there was never any worry over whether we could venture down any given road or trail. The innate assumption was that the land managed by the U.S. Forest Service or the National Park Service belonged to everyone and that finding our very own

little slice of heaven depended solely on how adventurous we were willing to be. And we were plenty adventurous.

As I grew up, I came to love the welcome signs to our national parks and our national forests. They symbolized the freedom we all knew we had but that few bothered to exercise. They signaled that adventure lay in wait, that, for days at a time, I could disappear into the woods and enjoy the things that made me whole. And there wasn't a damn thing anybody else could do about it. These places are sacred to me and to a lot of Americans who find peace, solitude and rejuvenation when we check out of our daily lives and turn to our birthright for rejuvenation.

In recent years, there has been a veiled movement on behalf of special interests in America to "transfer" public lands to states or sell them outright to private interests. Industrial development interests have been dark-money sources for coordinated campaigns that falsely claim that public lands are a management burden and that using them for extraction value is the only way to make them economically functional.

Other, more subtle elements, like the "patriots" who took over the Malhuer National Wildlife Refuge in January 2016, claim that federal ownership of land amounts to a land grab on the part of the government and that the land should be returned to its rightful private owners.

First, remember, the government doesn't own the land—you do. Second, the vast majority of public land in the United States was never owned by states or individuals. (Unless you consider the claims on the land from the nation's American Indian tribes that were in the West well before Lewis and Clark topped the Rockies and wandered all the way to the Pacific.) In fact, as a condition of statehood, most states in the undeveloped West had to give up any claims they might have had on land without private owners.

In other words, the "give it back" argument is based on the false assumption that public lands belonged to someone before they belonged to you. You need only remember that any effort to "transfer" or "sell" public

OPPOSITE, TOP: The moon rises over the lodgepoles on a chilly October evening atop Craig Pass. *Photo by Rachel Andona.*

OPPOSITE, BOTTOM: Jim Duke of Idaho Falls casts to brown trout on the Firehole River in October. *Photo by Chris Hunt.*

land amounts to theft, a very real attempt at a land grab, often purveyed by "useful idiots" like the Malheur Gang, who, likely unknowingly, are doing the dirty work of deep-pocketed extractors.

As someone who visits our national parks, national forests and national wildlife refuges, you need only know that you're a part of a national recreation economy worth $881 billion—which exceeds the oil, gas and mining industries that are often among the sale and transfer advocates. Your public lands are worth more to the American economy—some 2 percent of our annual GDP—left just as they are.

Now, that's not to say everything is perfect. It's not. Our land management agencies—which employ the folks who oversee the maintenance, repair and upkeep of our public lands—are woefully underfunded. The National Park Service, for instance, operated in fiscal year 2018 under a $2.6 billion budget (down almost $300 million from 2017). In 2004, the National Park Service operated under the same $2.6 billion budget. With inflation factored in, however, the park service operated on a budget more than $800 million smaller in 2018 than it did in 2004, despite the fact that national parks saw nearly sixty million more visitors in 2018 than in 2004.

Sadly, this is acceptable to politicians who allocate taxpayer money to fund our government from Washington, D.C. Equally unfortunate? We don't hold them accountable at the ballot box on this issue. Our birthright is under the care of some of the most talented and creative people in the country, but they're given a slumlord's budget to care for it.

When you visit Yellowstone and notice the cracked pavement on the Grand Loop Road, the outhouse that's about to overflow, the downed tree on the trail you're using to find the next stretch of fishy water or the general lack of infrastructure to handle the growing crowds, the increase in traffic and all the trappings that come with more than four million visitors a year, don't point a finger at the park service.

Don't blame the good people—those "damn government bureaucrats"—who work every day to ensure your safety and provide you with an experience you'll never forget. Call your member of Congress and let them know what you saw and how you feel about it. They approve the budget. Ask them to give your public lands the funding needed to keep them healthy and functional. Ask them to live up to the Organic Act of 1872, which formally created Yellowstone as the world's first national park. That act included the famous verbiage that is, still today, scrawled atop the Roosevelt Arch at the park's North Entrance: "For the benefit and enjoyment of the people."

Tell them that your birthright is worth more than they're spending on it, that national parks and national forests matter to you. Tell them how much you spent on gas, fishing gear, entrance fees, hotels, restaurants, camping equipment and the like. Tell them how far you drove to get there or how much you spent on plane tickets so you could share your public lands with your family. Tell them what it's worth to you to rebuild and repair magical places like Yellowstone.

Tell them you vote.

There's only one Yellowstone National Park.

And aren't you lucky? It belongs to you.

References

Arnold, Jeff L., Colleen R. Detjens, Brian D. Ertel, Michael E. Ruhl and Todd M. Koel. "West Slope Cutthroat Trout & Fluvial Arctic Grayling Restoration." *Yellowstone Science* 25, no. 1 (2017).

Kendall, W.C. *The Fishes of Yellowstone National Park.* Washington, D.C.: United States Bureau of Fisheries, 1914 and 1915.

Koel, Todd. "*An Approach to Conservation of Native Fish in Yellowstone, National Park Service.*" 2017.

Koel, Todd M., et al. *Predatory Fish Invasion Induces Within and Across Ecosystem Effects in Yellowstone National Park.* 2019.

———. Yellowstone National Park Native Fish Conservation Plan. 2010.

Merrill, Marlene Deahl. *Yellowstone and the Great West: Journals, Letters and Images from the 1871 Hayden Expedition.* Lincoln: University of Nebraska Press, 1999.

Montana Field Guides. http://fieldguide.mt.gov.

National Park Service Budget, 2004. https://www.nps.gov/upload/fy-2004-greenbook.pdf.

National Park Service Budget, 2018. https://www.nps.gov/aboutus/upload/FY-2018-NPS-Greenbook.pdf.

The National Recreation Economy Report. Boulder, CO: Outdoor Industry Association, 2017.

Park, R. *Fishing Yellowstone Park.* Guilford, CT: Falcon Publishing, 1988.

Schneider, B. *Hiking Yellowstone National Park.* 3rd ed. Guilford, CT: Falcon Publishing, 2013.

Schweber, N. *Fly Fishing Yellowstone National Park: An Insider's Guide to the 50 Best Places*. Mechanicsburg, PA: Stackpole Books, 2012.

Smith, Hugh M., and William C. Kendall. *The Fishes of Yellowstone National Park*. Washington, D.C.: Department of Commerce, 1921.

Van Kirk, R.W., J.M. Capurso and M.A. Novak, eds. "Exploring Differences between Fine-Spotted and Large-Spotted Yellowstone Cutthroat Trout." American Fisheries Society, Idaho Chapter, Caribou-Targhee National Forest, U.S. Bureau of Reclamation, Snake River Cutthroats Chapter of Trout Unlimited, 2006.

Varley, John D. *A History of Fish Stocking Activities in Yellowstone National Park between 1881 and 1980*. Washington, D.C.: National Park Service, U.S. Department of the Interior, 1981.

OTHER SOURCES

Associated Press.

Montana Angler Fly Fishing, 435 East Main Street, Bozeman, Montana, 59715.

National Park Service.

Orvis.

U.S. Geological Survey.

Yellowstone.net.

About the Author

C hris Hunt is an award-winning journalist, author and blogger who lives in Idaho Falls. He works and blogs for Trout Unlimited as the national digital director and is based in Idaho Falls, Idaho. His work has appeared in *TROUT* magazine, *Field & Stream*, the *New York Times*, the *Flyfish Journal*, *Hatch* magazine and several newspapers and magazines across the United States. This is his fourth book.

Author Chris Hunt on an October hike into Shoshone Lake via the DeLacy Creek Trail in search of lake trout. *Photo by Rachel Andona.*

Visit us at
www.historypress.com